MAKE FRIENDS WITH YOUR PERENNIALS AND BIENNIALS
JERRY BAKER

Designed and Edited by Charles Cook

Simon and Schuster   New York

We would like to thank the following individuals and organizations for providing the photographs which appear in this book:

Cook—6, 18, 29, 30, 34, 37, 47, 48, 50, 51, 55, 59, 64, 73; Garden Way Research—24; Orans—17, 72; Oregon Bulb Farms—28, 53; Pennsylvania State University Agricultural Extension Service—10; Roche—11; Wayside Gardens—15, 42; Wilkinson—4, 7, 8, 16, 21, 27, 32, 38, 45, 75.

Copyright © 1973 by Jerry Baker
All rights reserved
including the right of reproduction
in whole or in part in any form
Published by Simon and Schuster
Rockefeller Center, 630 Fifth Avenue
New York, New York 10020

SBN 671-21653-8 Paperback
Library of Congress Catalog Card Number: 73-8221
Designed by Charles Cook
Manufactured in the United States of America

1 2 3 4 5 6 7 8 9 10

Cover photo by Geo. W. Park Seed Co., Inc.

Contents

5 Perennial Friends

7 Uses

16 Site

25 Soil

27 Feeding

29 Planting

45 Beds

50 Care

53 Feeding

61 Pests

66 Propagation

74 Biennials

77 Guide to Perennials and Biennials

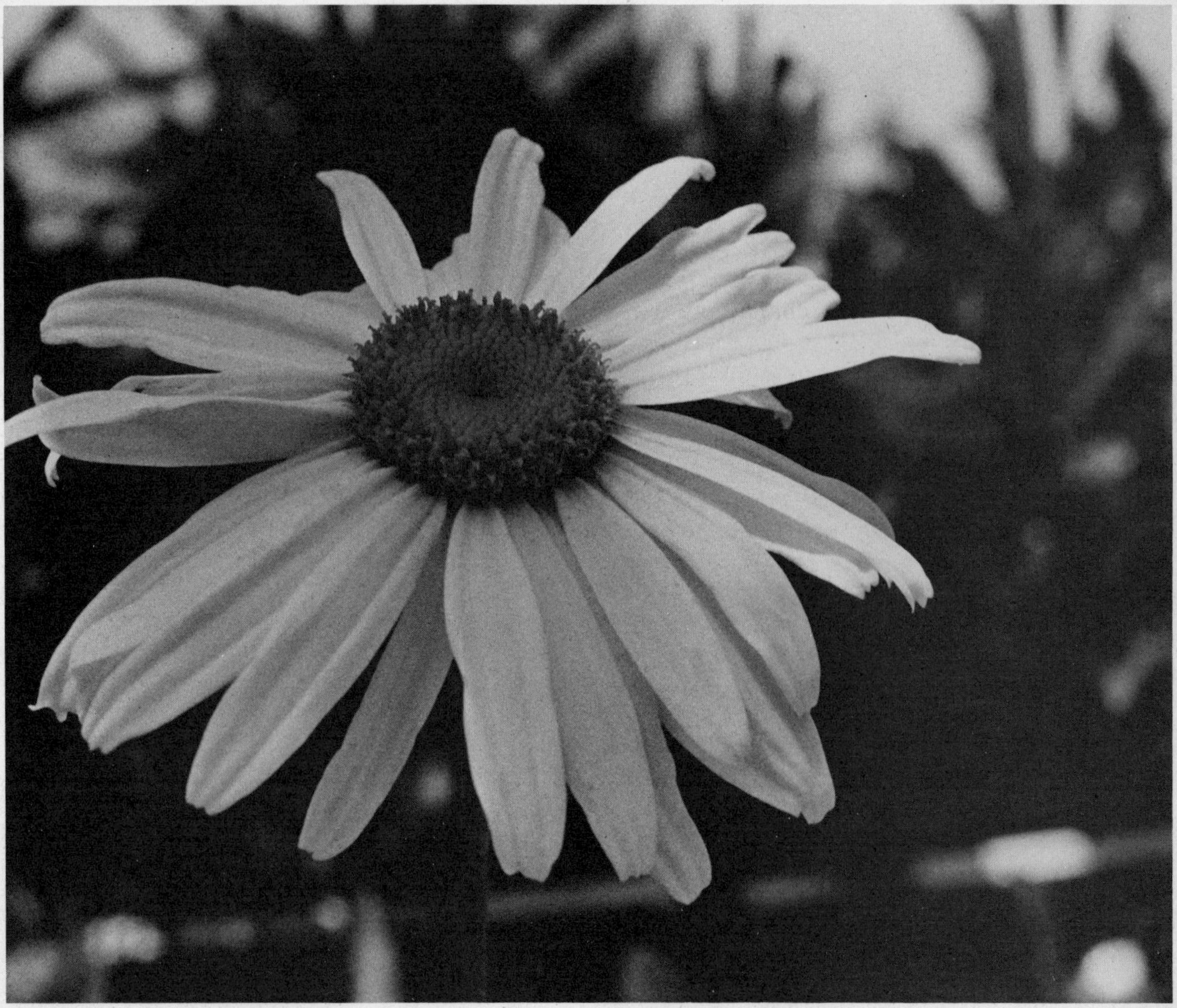

Perennials are tough

Perennial Friends

Perennials are flowers with character. They are not fair-weather friends. They do not tremble, shrivel and fall over when the first cool winds of autumn blow against their startled faces. They do not leave the scene abruptly never to return again. No indeed, perennials are fellows you can put your trust in.

True, some of them may lose their leaves or temporarily go underground to rest and renew their strength. I understand their need for this and never question their loyalty. I know that when spring comes again, they will thrust their heads through the winter mulch. They will delight me for another season, partners in beauty with all the other flowering plants in my landscape, working hand in hand with annuals, shrubs, trees and vines.

For perennials are sturdy fellows. No less handsome than other members of the community, they are more to be relied upon than the annuals, take less room than most shrubs and trees, and do not ramble all over the place like the vines. But, secure in their worth and supremely confident, they work cooperatively with all the others, keeping order in the garden with a firm but kindly hand.

Our reliance in each other is mutual — they look to me for care. I try not to disappoint them, and to be worthy of their trust. I feed, water, mulch and divide them as the need arises. They, to show their appreciation, tend diligently to business, performing their assigned tasks with care and precision.

If you would enjoy working with perennials toward the common good, you must first understand exactly what a perennial is. They are flowering foliage plants whose roots live on from year to year. Their tops may, or may not, die back in the winter, largely depending on the section of the country where they live. In the North, they may die back and some should have their roots well protected with a mulch in winter; in the South they may be evergreen.

Among their many good qualities is the color they give to my garden in shady spots and in front of the evergreen. They are bright and cheerful in spring and throughout the growing season.

I count on my perennials to flower before other types of plants. Some are so eager that they flower the first year after planting.

Perennials of this type may be grown as annuals if you prefer, thus eliminating the problems of winter protection.

But, generally speaking, perennials will not flower until they have reached a certain size, are then exposed to low temperature for a number of weeks, and then exposed to increasing day lengths and increasing temperatures. Their flowering time is the result of this sequence of day length and temperature.

Another thing that makes perennials so valuable is their persistence. Once you have secured a "start" or division, they soon become truly permanent residents, returning each year with renewed vitality. They complain very seldom, have built-in good health, and are willing to take on any job you decide to give them. Provided, of course, they are suited to the task.

That's why you must be careful in their selection. I always plan to keep my perennials around for a long, long time. I don't like discharging one of them because I made a mistake in judgment when I invited him to my home in the first place. And the error is wholly mine, for he is not a pushy fellow — I have never known a member of his family to move in unasked, unlike the annuals whose "seedy" children frequently dance over on the wind from my neighbor's garden.

Check with your nurseryman or talk with some long time resident in your area whose garden you admire. Check your prospective guest's credentials and performance record before you invite him in. This one step can save you a lot of grief. Climate plays an important part. He may be sturdy and completely reliable in some areas, but too-cold winter or too-hot summer may so affect his health that he simply cannot cope with the assignment you have in mind for him, try as he will. Plants are very much like people. Some are stronger than others, some taller, some shorter. Think ahead and decide what you expect of him and then choose a willing worker who is equal to the task — someone who will dive right into the job ahead and give you the help you are looking for.

An established clump of perennials like this one will grace a garden for years to come.

Perennials yield a tremendous harvest of beauty with a minimum of upkeep.

Having made your selection, remember that you must give him elbow room — this boy will very likely expand his activities as time goes on. With plenty of living space, he won't feel crowded. If he is a member of one of the really hard-working, fast-growing groups, like the irises or day lilies, he's going to want to stretch out from time to time, and you may have to curb him a little.

If he is a really fine fellow—and you aren't going to invite any other kind, are you? — turn his overenthusasm to your advantage. Consider this as his way of "paying as he goes," giving you sturdy offspring to plant elsewhere, to give away to friends, or even to sell.

Uses

Once you've chosen perennials suited to your climate, fellows who will require a minimum of care and upkeep, you can plant them just about anywhere. Naturalize them in a woodland near your home if you like. They can be particularly attractive in such a setting and require little care.

I cannot emphasize too much or too frequently the necessity of choosing plants that are suited to the spot you place them in. To have them become almost life-long companions, you must see to their care and comfort from the very beginning. Help them to feel secure and at home, just as you would do for a loved one who came to live with you. Help them to get established — and don't forget to introduce them around to the neighbors. If you plant perennials under trees, they will have to learn to understand their giant companions and to share from the very beginning. The shade of the trees will limit the perennials you can grow in that particular area. Also the roots of some large trees are quite greedy of all the available moisture.

Since the trees will quite likely be there before the perennials, consider the type and

Formal plantings should be carefully planned and neat, not monotonous and stiff.

kind of tree you and your perennial pal are going to have to deal with. If it is a deep-rooted tree, you will have more scope, but if it is a type with many surface feeder roots, they will be competing with your perennials, which may come out second unless you do something to help. Simply see that neither the tree nor your newly arrived friend suffers for want of food or water.

Shade will be another deciding factor as to what you can and cannot grow. Plants that do well in shade or partial shade include ageratum, bleeding heart, columbine, coral bells, forget-me-not, foxglove, and violas, to mention but a few.

Also consider using wildflowers native to your area. Many grow in woodlands, and if you give them similar soil conditions, they will thrive in your naturalized garden area under the shade of the trees. Wood anemones and hepaticas can be very lovely. Violets grow wild in many places and, once established, are very charming as they increase and return year after year.

Perennials with a Sunny Disposition

So much for a naturalistic setting. Just suppose you do not have trees and rocks, but have chosen to live in a house largely surrounded by sunny open spaces. There are a great many perennials that enjoy living in just such a location, and you will enjoy having them do so.

Perhaps the best way to combine your desire for neatness and your longing for great masses of bloom is to have a formal planting along your walks, driveway and foundation. This formal planting will need more care — you will have to devote a little more time to keeping it attractive at all seasons.

Farther out in the yard, you can really let yourself go, planting or sowing seed in great random-shaped patches if you like. A sunny area will not necessarily have poor soil, but this is likely, and since it is often impractical to fertilize such a large area, you should take this problem into consideration.

Also, there is the matter of watering. If you live in a hot, dry climate, you must choose perennials that can stand up and take it year after year without dying out when summer sun strikes, even though they may not continue to flourish at their springtime best when this season arrives.

Plants which will do well in most areas in dry or poor soils, include centaureas such as perennial bachelor's buttons or dusty millers, four o'clocks, gaillardias, irises, lupines, Oriental poppies, and pampas grass.

Water, Water Everywhere

A wet spot can be handled several different ways. Before I consign any of my new friends to live in such a place, I always carefully consider the character of the area. Is the wet spot shady or sunny? Is it beside a stream or in a bog? What is the soil like?

Of all the possibilities, I think planting beside a brook or small stream can be one of life's greatest joys — so it should not be undertaken lightly. Consider color, height, length of blooming season and all factors pertinent to perennial pleasure—and yours.

The brilliant yellow marsh marigold may be an excellent choice. Astilbe is another perennial which thrives best in a soil that is constantly moist. Yellow flag irises naturalize well in a moist location. Other possibilities include forget-me-nots, foxglove, sweet violets and violas. All of these will do well in moist, shady, or semi-shady spots — but your wet spot may be in full sun. What then? There are still some pretty perennials who will be delighted to come in and take charge, such as rose mallow and blue flag iris. Give them a chance to "do their thing," and see how eagerly they'll dive in and bring beauty to an otherwise unsightly area where nothing else wants to grow.

Many perennials love to dabble their toes in the cool water of a stream or pool.

Perennial ground covers can solve a lot of problems beautifully.

So you have a steep bank, difficult to mow and subject to soil erosion with every rain. Perennials will move in again and do what's necessary to hold things together. Plant trailing periwinkle (Vinca minor), or creeping lily-turf. Help them to get established, then you can forget the whole thing except on those occasions when you stop and admire the beauty of the scene. At such times, don't forget to give them a few words of praise for the fine job they are doing. As stewards of that particular section, they will want to know from time to time that you are pleased, even though they know that you are trusting them to do well and carry out your orders without constant supervision.

Shady soil is apt to be acid. Of course, some perennials will be perfectly at home under such conditions, but if you add lime to the soil you can broaden your choices. This need not be done too often. Once every three years is often enough, for most perennials will do reasonably well in soil that is somewhat acid.

Never plant in a shady location any perennials that require full sun. It will be a waste of your time and theirs and there will be disappointment all around. Irises, for instance, which grow gloriously in full sun, will be tall and spindly and may even refuse to bloom in the shade.

But, you say, a cool, shady place makes a wonderful retreat on a hot summer day, and you want something that will bloom there too. And I agree with you. Consider hostas, sometimes called by the silly name of funkia. Plantain lily, another name for this lovely flower, sounds much better and is far more descriptive. Hostas make a clump of large-leaved lilies, and they were very popular years ago. In old gardens, traces of them sometimes remain long after the old house is gone. The lilies themselves are large, waxy white and very fragrant. These late

"Trouble at the border? Let me handle it, partner!"

summer flowers are very large, 4 to 6 inches long, and are borne above the clumps of shiny, light green, heart-shaped leaves. Solid masses of these are extremely attractive, or you may use them to border your woodland path.

Most perennials do not grow as tall as shrubs, yet they may be used very effectively as screens, especially those Texas-tall types like delphiniums and hollyhocks, for instance.

If you live in a hot, dry climate, choose some real cowboys, like yucca or eremurus (giant desert-candle), who will be completely at home under a sizzling Western sun. They won't even need to wear sombreros. The tall spires of Yucca blossoms are often several feet long, and the white or cream-colored flowers are of breath-taking beauty.

Eremurus, sometimes called the Foxtail lilies are generally hardy up to New York and southern New England. They are not commonly seen and deserve to be better known, for they are truly spectacular, especially if planted as a screen. Try it sometime. They vary in color from white through shades of yellow, pink and peach.

Hollyhocks, as your grandmother well knew, are trustworthy and do nicely just about anywhere. This bright, cheerful, and obliging plant will quickly form a desirable screen in almost any section of the country. Delphiniums, on the other hand, will be more comfortable in cooler, moister climates. These aristrocrats of the garden are well worth a bit of extra trouble, and if you grow them you should exercise every care all through the summer. Weed, cultivate and water as necessary. If you are just starting a young planting, be sure to spade the soil deeply, fertilize well, and give them a sunny location.

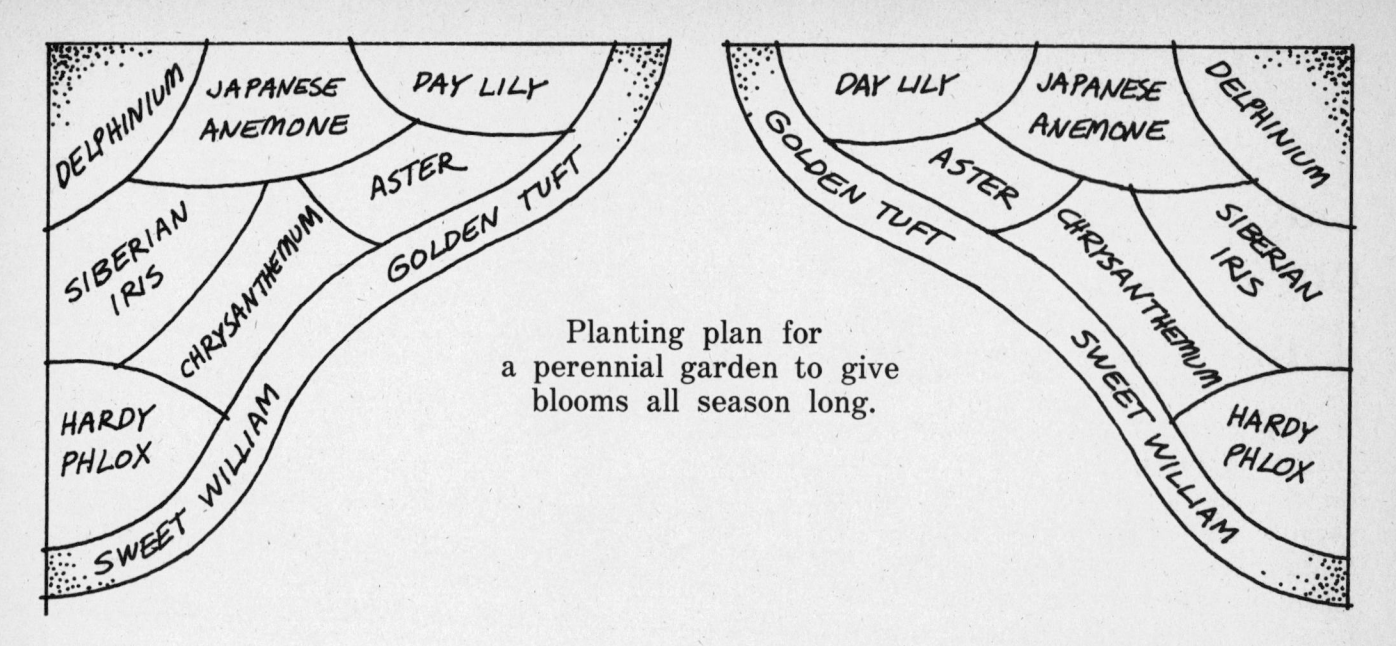

Planting plan for a perennial garden to give blooms all season long.

Keeping Order at the Border

The most attractive perennial borders are formed by grouping together plants of the same type, not necessarily of the same variety. Careful planning will enable you to arrange these so that there is always something in bloom all along the border.

Something else to consider is your color scheme. I try to plan this far in advance to prevent strong, positive colors from clashing with each other. You can elaborate on this idea by having the lighter, pastel shades earlier in the season, with the gay, sparkling blossoms more in evidence in late spring and summer.

Plants in small groups are always more effective than scattered individual plantings. Some of the larger perennials which tend to form large clumps, such as peonies, day lilies, asters or irises, can be planted individually. These are also quite apt to be the crowders. They do not really mean to be pushy but they are so gay and strong and full of vitality that they are likely to quickly grow beyond the space you told them to stay in. When this happens, they are apt to overshadow some of the more delicate plants — possibly some of the loveliest — so you may have to give them a stern "talking to" from time to time. If they are multiplying very rapidly, let them pioneer new territory somewhere else in your landscape, or naturalize the extras in a nearby woods or meadow. Divide and let them conquer.

Let them grow during the summer. I like to just watch and make a few notes. Then, in late summer or early fall, I know exactly what I want to do. Then, when I have the time, I get busy. I try not to wait too long, however, for even these hardy boys need to have a chance to make new roots and get themselves securely fastened down before frost. If they don't, the alternate freezing and thawing of the ground in winter may prove to be too much even for their strong constitutions.

Fall is the time too for planning another border beauty look-ahead—the bulbs. Springflowering bulbs are charming with the early border perennials, making a magic carpet around their feet. Most of them claim their share of attention and then retire gracefully from the scene, just as the later perennials step out onto the stage.

Cut Yourself in on a Beautiful Thing

If your garden area is confined to the usual, rather small city lot, you will probably not have room for a second garden especially for supplying cut flowers for indoor use. Sometimes it is almost a heartbreaking choice to make—whether you will let the flowers continue to bloom on the plant, or cut a few choice blossoms to take as a gift to a friend, or simply to dress up the dining table for a festive occasion.

But even with the smallest lot, there are still choices. I remember once when I lived in a house with a postage-stamp-size yard. A family celebration was being planned and we just had to have some flowers. I shut my eyes and robbed one of the perennials (the only one that happened to have blossoms at that particular moment) of nearly all its blooms. The happy occasion came and went, but when the flowers faded I did not throw them away. I reasoned that they were cuttings, and I had nothing to lose by trying an experiment.

I treated the base of the cuttings with a root stimulant, cut off the flower heads but left on all the remaining foliage. Inserted in a homemade propagating frame and kept moist, they began to grow. As roots developed, I potted them up individually and gradually moved them from a shady location to full sun. The sunny spot happened to be a long, rather narrow space on the side of the garage. The flowers were largely out of sight, added little or nothing to the overall landscaping plan, but as they grew and flourished, I had a little, partially hidden cutting garden that gave me a great many blossoms and a lot of pleasure.

For lots of bloom, elect perennials for your particular area. Plan so you will be able to choose plants that will blossom together and also plants that will flower when there is nothing else in bloom.

But remember that many factors enter into the blooming of a plant at any particular time. The season may be wet and cold, and blossoming may be delayed. The flowering time may vary as much as six weeks from year to year, but plants of the same kind usually flower at the same time. However, the irises in my north front yard nearly always bloom a week later than those by my terrace, which get the full benefit of the western sun in the afternoon.

Here is a list of perennials that make very good cut flowers:

Anemone	Hosta
Aquilegia	Iris
Artemisia	Liatris
Campanula	Lupines
Centaurea	Nepeta
Chrysanthemum	Papaver
Coreopsis	Penstemon
Delphinium	Rudbeckia
Dianthus	Salvia
Digitalis	Scabiosa
Gaillardia	Viola
Gypsophila	
Helianthus	
Hemerocallis	

"Don't you think I'm a divine house guest, darling?"

How to Keep the Bloom in Youth

When cutting perennials, use sharp scissors or small pruning shears. Make a clean cut — a ragged one invites disease or insects. Carry a container along with you in which you have placed a small amount of water. Do not cut at random. Plan where you will use the flowers before you cut. This, of course, also includes the type of container in which they will be displayed. For the dining table you may want to use a low bowl, so cut your blossoms with short stems. A tall vase must be planned for accordingly or the flowers will disappear from view when placed in it.

Garden flowers actually have several advantages over those bought from the florist. The first time you cut some of your own, you may be in for a delightful surprise. For one thing, their stems are usually stronger. Florists like to make a nice display and usually show open or partially open flowers. You can cut yours while they are in the bud stage and have all the pleasure of watching them unfold, prolonging their period of usefulness and your own enjoyment. Remember further that you do not need to cut a huge bouquet. Just a few blooms can make an attractive arrangement.

You may find that such aids as pinholders, small stakes and ties will assist you in working up a design. To keep your flowers fresh as long as possible, try charring them at the stem end. This works particularly well with the gorgeous Oriental poppies that bloom in the spring—the big red ones. Flowers that have woody stems will often retain their freshness longer if they are hammered an inch or two at the cut end so they can absorb more water.

Learning to arrange flowers takes quite a bit of time and effort, but the results make it all worthwhile.

Flower arranging is an art which takes time and effort to learn, and some trial and error on your part may be necessary before you achieve the effect you are seeking. But it is always a pleasurable experience and no arrangement is forever. There is always a next time, and we all learn gradually from our mistakes. Don't mourn too much if things didn't turn our exactly right — enjoy your blossoms anyhow. Above all, smile at them as you pass, it wasn't their fault and they shouldn't be made to shoulder any part of the blame!

Of course you can combine perennials with perennials, or perennials with bulbs, annuals or flowering shrubs. Those of us who do not have large yards generally use what is available at any particular season. But knowing a few basic rules may help.

A Few Basic Rules

There should always be a "main line," and the most successful arrangements usually come if you plan this first of all, thus forming a skeleton for the rest of the structure. Let strong lines set the pattern for the design and all the rest will come later. Sometimes foliage is more useful for this purpose than flowers.

There should be harmony between the container, the foliage and the flowers. Having decided in advance upon the container you will use, you will find that it's easy to choose and cut flowers well suited to it.

Flower arrangements should always have a center of interest. Clever designers know exactly what first attracts the eye when we glance at a display. First we notice the tips, buds or foliage at the highest point, then the eye travels downward to finally arrive at its destination—the focal point of the arrangement. This should be the most perfect and colorful blossom you happen to have at the moment.

Site

The amount of light which your perennials receive is largely determined by their proximity to other plants and structures. Neighboring buildings, large shade trees, or fences may make it very difficult to give them all they need to grow and flourish. Still you must make the effort. Sun-loving irises will not do well in shade; they must have the warmth of the sun on the rhizomes for long periods to flower with color and flair.

But do not be discouraged if you have a shady lawn. There are perennials for all sections, seasons and occasions. They comprise one of the largest and most lavishly flowering families in the whole plant kingdom. Take sedums, for instance. This is a sturdy plant with small flowers borne in broad heads on erect leafy stems, 1 to 2 feet tall. The colors are usually rose-pink but may be white or purple. They bloom from mid-August well into October. This obliging fellow will fulfill just about any need you may have. They grow on virtually all soils. And, though some of his tribe prefer full sunshine, there are other nephews, cousins and uncles who will grow in shade as well. Just don't put him in a wet spot where water can stand and settle around his feet — that he doesn't like.

Some trees and shrubs are the cause of shady situations. If you don't like the bare spots under them, use a good ground cover such as leadwort, plantain lilies or candytuft. But beware! Think well before you introduce them to the rest of the garden inhabitants — they can be real take-over mobsters, spreading in an astonishing fashion and often muscling in where they are least wanted.

rights so you must help them to get along together just as family members do. Keep the perennials in bounds so that they do not shade the lower branches of the shrubs and cause them to drop their leaves. Do plant them a sufficient distance apart so each can have breathing space and ample sunshine.

Perennials are over-achievers; they often grow right out of their beds.

How to Avoid Growing Pains

Where perennials and shrubs or trees are planted adjacent to each other, it is necessary to look ahead and give consideration to the size both will eventually attain. If, for instance, you are planning a perennial bed with a hedge for its background, you should allow at least 3 feet of space between the two. Both should have ample room to grow and develop. Allowance should be made for good air circulation, and you should have room to clip and prune the hedge as the need arises.

Perennials, happy and secure in a comfortable spot, have a way of growing exuberantly and may, in an innocent burst of enthusiasm, march over the edges of their beds. You can prepare for this by allowing them some spill space. This can be a broad edging such as a garden path or a low wall of stone or brick.

It's a very good idea to plant day lilies as an edging for a perennial border where the bed fronts on a lawn. The high-growing foliage fountains out gracefully, and it obligingly moves to the side when the lawn mower is brought close to the bed for trimming.

The shrubs, trees and perennials in your yard are all your children and all have equal

Snub Sneaky Shrubs

The shrubs must learn that the perennials have their rights also. You can help them to understand this by carefully pruning out any branches which lean over the perennials, shading them out and interfering with their normal growth. Tell the shrub to curb his curiosity about what his neighbor is doing and not to be so nosey.

Now that you know what inquisitive fellows shrubs are, remember that they are apt to go rambling around under the ground as well. A little root pruning may be in order from time to time — especially if you catch him slipping over into the perennial bed. In all likelihood he will be better off himself and develop more feeder roots. Cut in a circle, or semi-circle, at the weep line of the tree or shrub.

Even the smallest home grounds have room for a few perennials. They are fine for bordering paths and they mix in well with bulbs and annuals, supplying a long season of color and foliage after the bulbs and annuals have stopped blossoming. A good trick is to plant annuals directly over the bulbs so they can take their place when the bulb foliage dies. This two-level gardening will keep everything uncrowded but lovely all year long.

Good soil preparation is the first step to success with perennials.

Preparing the soil is extremely important to the future good conduct of your perennials. For, while annuals will often grow and flower in poorly prepared soil, perennials seldom survive more than a year or so if good preparation has been neglected.

Soil, properly prepared, will have good drainage, protection from drying winds, and adequate water in the summer. If you prepare the beds with care by spading deeply, providing adequate drainage, and lightening up the heavy soil with sand and organic matter, you can be almost certain of success.

Water enters and moves through well-prepared soil easily. So do those little helpers of Mother Nature, the earthworms, whose movements aerate the soil and whose castings enrich it. Seed will germinate readily, and the plants will quickly grow deep, healthy root systems and strong, sturdy stems. The blossoms will be large and abundant. Furthermore, the benefits of careful soil preparation carry over from season to season.

Especially if you are a new gardener, don't get carried away. Grandiose dreams by the fireside will eventually have to give way to practical considerations. In other words, don't bite off more than you can chew. Gardening just ceases to be fun when you have to work at it constantly, so cut everything down to size. It is far better to grow a small bed of flowers in well-prepared soil than to attempt to grow great masses of flowers in poorly prepared soil.

There will always be another spring. Next year — and success will give you confidence — you can plan a larger planting.

"The first thing you should learn is that I demand a nicely made bed."

Avoid Water Beds

You can get a jump on things by preparing the soil in the fall. You will also have all winter to figure out what you are going to plant in the allotted space.

Before you prepare any new beds, test the soil to see that it is capable of absorbing water from rainfall. A heavy clay soil may be almost impenetrable. And the soil must have water-holding capacity so that the plants will be able to fulfill their needs for moisture.

To test, dig a hole about 10 inches deep and fill it with water. The following day, fill the hole with water again and check to see how long the water remains in the hole. If it drains away in 8 to 10 hours the permeability of the soil is adequate for the plants to make good growth. However, if a quantity of water is still in the hole after 10 hours, you will need to improve the drainage of the planting site. If you don't, water will stand in the flower bed and prevent proper development of the roots.

To improve matters, bed up the soil. Dig furrows along the sides of the bed and add the soil from the furrows to the bed. This has the general effect of raising the level of the soil. And excess water can seep from the bed into the furrows.

Gullies in raised beds may become apparent after heavy rains. This can be prevented by surrounding the beds with wooden or masonry walls, making raised planters of the beds. Old railroad ties, if they can be obtained, are excellent for this purpose.

Bear in mind that raised beds will dry out more quickly than flat beds, for little moisture will move up into the bed from the soil below. More frequent watering will be necessary during the summer. This bit of extra care is offset by the fact that you don't have to stoop so far when doing the weeding.

Let's Get Down to Earth

After making the beds or deciding that drainage is satisfactory without raising them, spade the soil to a depth of 8 to 10 inches. Turn it over completely. And while you are doing this, remove any boards, large stones or building trash that may be buried. Do yourself a favor and keep a cardboard box or bushel basket handy.

Discard the trash, but turn under all leaves, grass, stems, roots and anything else that will quickly and easily decay. Repeat this spading operation three or four times at weekly intervals. If the soil becomes dry between spadings, water it. If weeds grow, pull

A rototiller is good for turning under leaves, grass and other organic matter.

them out. Don't let them set seed.

In spring, just before planting time, spade again. Now is the time to work in peat moss, sand and fertilizer. Adding some agricultural lime to the soil will also be of benefit.

Your soil is probably "ordinary garden soil". For this, I would recommend a 1-to-2-inch layer of peat moss and a 1-inch layer of unwashed sand, the kind usually found at building supply yards.

If what you have is heavy clay, double the amount of peat and sand. Continue to add peat and sand to the soil each time you reset the plants, and you will eventually improve even poor subsoil, transforming it into good garden loam—that almost mythical stuff that all gardeners dream about. Well-rotted compost will be fine to use instead of peat moss.

I once had a diligent friend who hand dug a well down to a depth of a little more than 20 feet. The subsoil brought up from this depth was placed on the surface and thoughtlessly spread over a wide area. When he became aware of the growth impediment it was presenting, he started practicing soil enrichment according to the program outlined above and in a year or two you wouldn't have recognized that soil. The dense, heavy, yellow clay even changed color, becoming dark, rich and friable.

A Toast to Compost

Every gardener should have a compost heap, for compost provides one of the easiest and cheapest ways to increase the fertility of your garden. And a heap is a handy place to dispose of most of your garden waste, such as dead foliage, vegetable tops and peelings, grass clippings and other plant material that will rot quickly. Just don't put in any diseased plant material — burn or otherwise dispose of it.

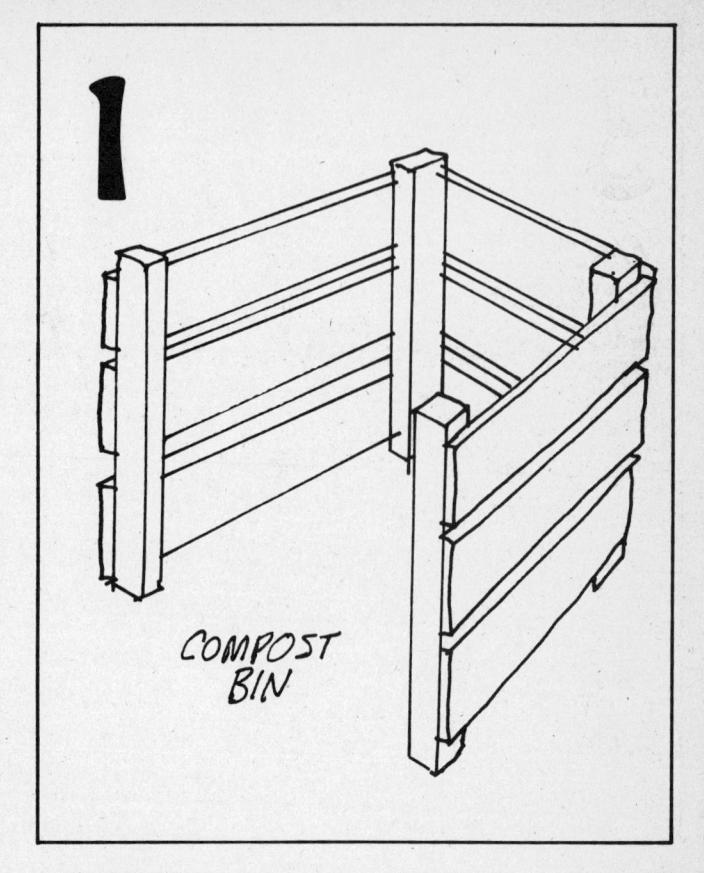

3 — WASTE; LIME, FERTILIZER AND SOIL; WASTE; WASTE

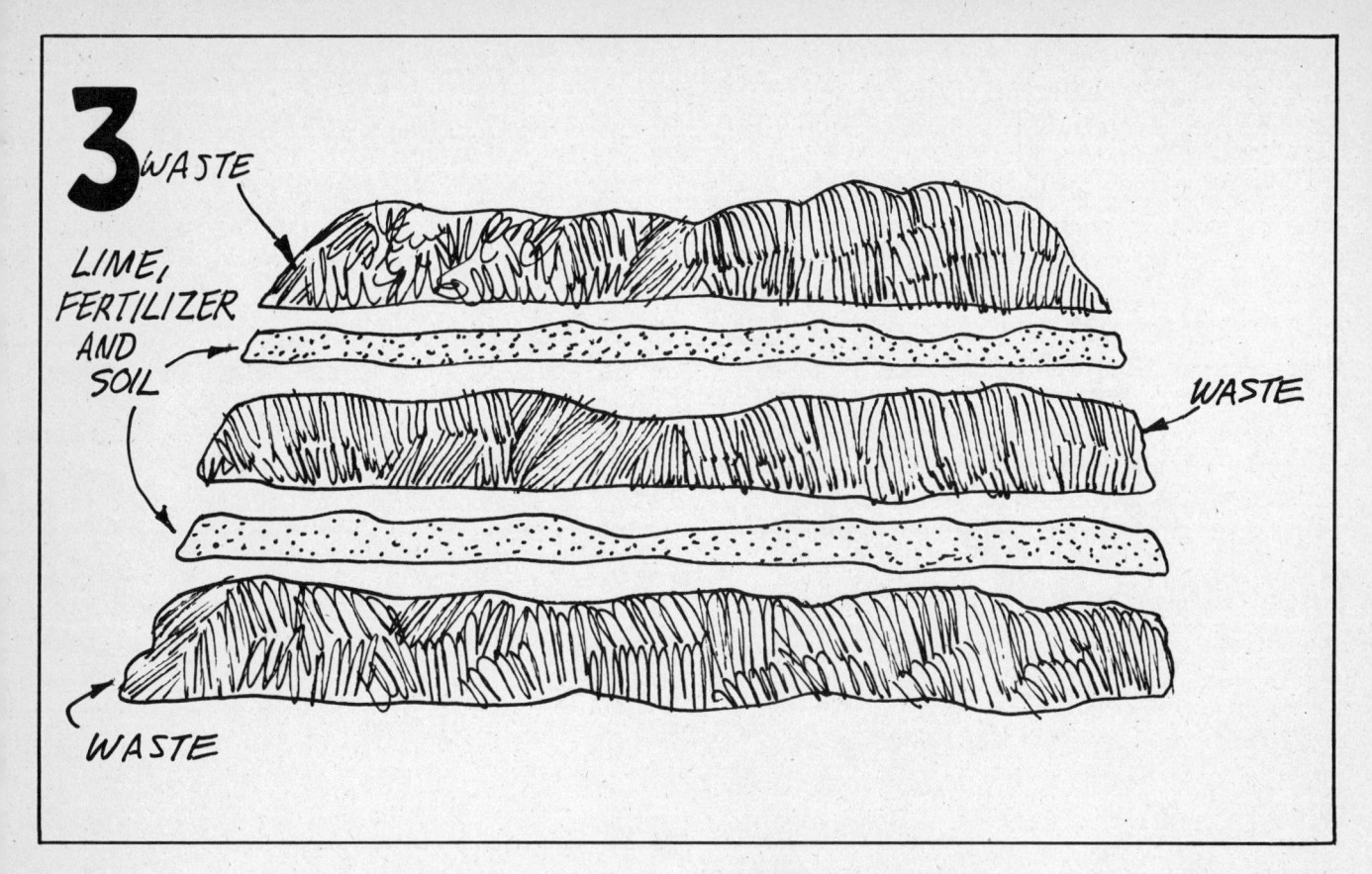

1. Make your compost bin 3 to 4 feet tall and wide and as long as you need. The sides may be built of concrete blocks, old doors or lumber.

2. Put in a 6-inch layer of plant material.

3. Sprinkle with lime and barnyard manure or 5-10-15. Add a layer of soil and wet down the heap. Repeat this layering until the pile is complete.

4. Make the center of the pile concave to allow rainwater to collect. Drive a stake into the heap to provide good aeration. Keep the heap moist at all times.

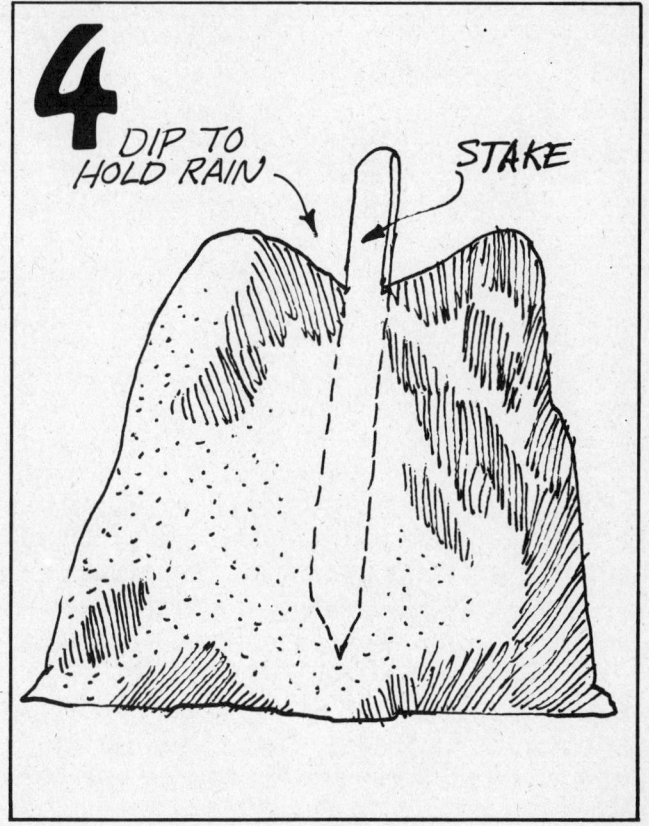

4 — DIP TO HOLD RAIN; STAKE

Build your heap 3 to 4 feet tall and as wide and long as your needs dictate. Line the sides with boards. If you have plenty of room, you can use cement blocks — which may prove to be less expensive with the price of lumber rising by leaps and bounds. You could use old doors for the sides or lumber from an old building or fence.

Put in a 6-inch layer of plant material. Sprinkle this layer with lime and barnyard manure, if available. If not, use 5-10-5 fertilizer — one cup to a square yard of litter.

Add a thin layer of soil to keep the litter in place and thoroughly moisten. Repeat this layering as often as you accumulate enough plant material until the pit is filled. If kitchen wastes are used, be sure to cover with enough soil each time to keep down flies and odors.

As you build, make the center lower than the sides, thus allowing natural rainfall to seep down into the litter. Water as often as necessary to keep the compost moist, paying particular attention to this during the hot, dry summer months when natural rainfall is likely to be scanty.

After about 3 or 4 months, turn the contents of the pit from top to bottom, mixing it thoroughly. Or you can drive a stake into the heap to provide the necessary aeration.

Materials composted in this manner will be ready for use the following spring. Remove and use or, better still, start a second pit. That way you will have one pit with compost ready to use, and one pit to use for composting fresh material as it accumulates.

You can also compost under shrubs and in the back of flower beds. If the composting material is covered with hay, pine needles or peat moss, it will not be unsightly.

Adding organic matter to your soil will:

Make a heavy (particularly clay) soil lighter, causing it to become crumbly and friable.

Help light soil particles hold together and anchor them against erosion.

Provide the nitrogen needed by plants in a readily usable form.

Help release nutrients already present in the soil by turning them into soluble compounds that are more easily absorbed by plant roots.

Permit growth and functioning of micro-organisms.

Supply a small quantity of all elements essential for plant growth.

Let's be fair, here is what it won't do:

It will not reduce infestations of weeds.

It will not diminish plant diseases. Never, I repeat never, put diseased plant materials in the compost pit.

Soil

It is important to know the type of soil you are dealing with before you decide what you are going to plant in it. You can probably determine quickly whether it is clayey or sandy, but the degree of acidity or alkalinity and the proportions of humus, nitrogen, potash and phosphorus will not be so readily apparent. A simple soil test will determine these factors and can be made quickly and inexpensively by taking a soil sample to your county agent or sending it to your state experiment station.

You must collect your soil samples correctly; if the sample is not representitive of the area, the test can be misleading and the results and recommendations will be incorrect. Also, when sending your sample to the experiment station, state clearly that you are planning to grow flowers in the soil. And be sure to allow sufficient time between sending in your sample and your need for the information.

Start by obtaining copies of the correct form from your county agent. Fill out a form for each composite sample you wish to have tested. Take your soil samples with a probe, spade, garden trowel or soil auger. You will also need a bucket for mixing samples and a box, sack or fruit jar for holding one pint of mixed soil. Collect a composite sample. This means a mixture of several borings or spade slices from one sampled area. Clear away trash, if any, on top of the soil before taking samples. Don't take soil samples when the ground is wet.

How often should you test? Once every 3 to 5 years is usually enough.

About 65% of all soil samples are submitted to state laboratories for testing during the months of March, April, August and September. You will probably obtain faster service if you submit your samples either before or after these months! Samples can be collected at any time when the soil is

"Ah, this soil is just right. Not too acid and not too alkaline."

dry and in suitable condition. Don't wait until just before planting time.

But if you just happen to be forgetful and want a soil test made in a hurry, there is still a way out. Follow the basic rules outlined and take your own soil sample. Buy one of the many soil testing kits now on the market and follow the directions carefully.

Can Your Soil Pass the Acid Test?

After you have had your soil tested, or made the test yourself, what are you going to do about the results? Understanding them is the first step. The pH of soil is simply its active acidity or alkalinity expressed in units. Shade-loving plants generally prefer an acid soil; sun-loving plants prefer an alkaline one.

Whether you will tip the balance a little toward acidity or alkalinity depends on what you intend to grow.

Most soils, as you continue to add compost, peat moss, and other organic matter, will tend to become more acid. If in time it becomes apparent that you need to neutralize the acidity, add lime to your soil. Lime added to your compost heap may be sufficient to maintain a correct soil balance.

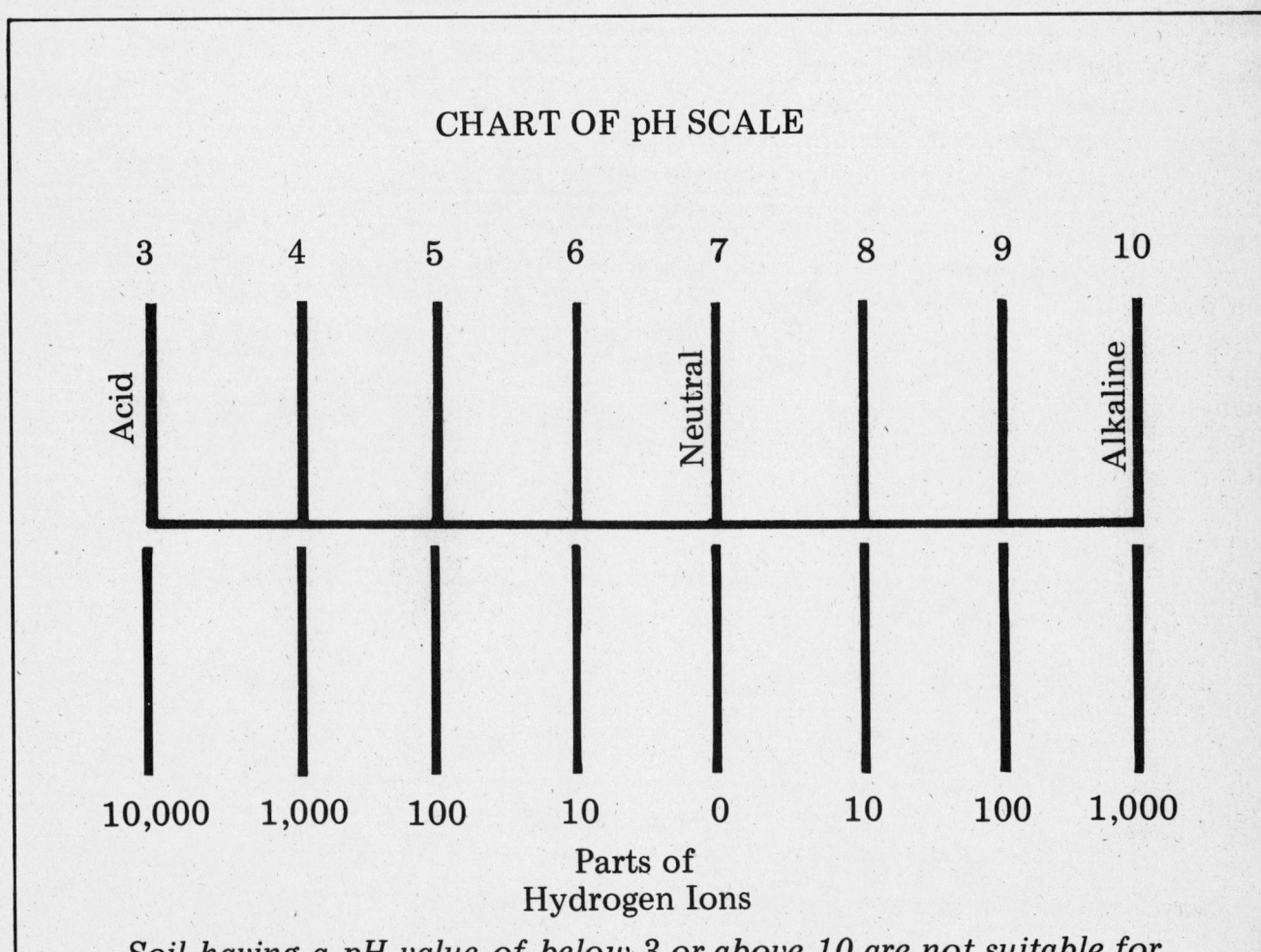

CHART OF pH SCALE

3	4	5	6	7	8	9	10
Acid				Neutral			Alkaline
10,000	1,000	100	10	0	10	100	1,000

Parts of Hydrogen Ions

Soil having a pH value of below 3 or above 10 are not suitable for gardening or growing crops.

Perennials need regular but light doses of fertilizer to stay in top condition.

Feeding

Fertilization must be done regularly to keep the soil fertile. The long growing seasons of perennials soon rob it of its natural fertility.

Never fertilize perennials heavily with inorganic fertilizers. Practice light fertilization with a continuous supply rather than occasional big doses. This will produce plants that are easier to train or support on stakes, and the plants will not have foliage so dense that it interferes with air circulation.

If your soil is high in organic content or becomes so in time from the use of much peat moss or compost, you can fertilize with 5-10-5. Put little rings of fertilizer around each plant in early spring. Repeat this six weeks later, and again six weeks after that. In all probability, this will be sufficient to carry the plants through the summer.

But don't neglect the late-blooming boys. Apply fertilizer in late summer or early fall and just watch them take a new interest in life!

Always water the bed after applying fertilizer. This washes the fertilizer off the foliage, thus preventing fertilizer burn, and makes the fertilizer available to the plant. Don't let him sit there hungrily eyeing food he can't eat. The fertilizer must enter the soil; no matter how long it stays on the surface, it will not be available to the plant. It must get down to where his roots can find it.

Remember—plan a program. Fertilize regularly, a little at a time. Your perennials will appreciate this and show it by looking their best all through the season, both in and out of bloom.

After plants are set out or thinned, cultivate only to break crusts on the surface of the soil. When the plants start to grow, stop cultivating altogether. In limited areas, weeds should be pulled by hand—frequently.

Rake fertilizer into the ground well so it can get to the roots.

Some perennials may be grown from seed; others may be purchased as plants at garden centers like the one below.

Planting

Don't be in a rush to start seeds or to set out started plants. I know you are eager to get started and it's easy to be lured into activity on the first deceptively warm day of spring. But hold on! Delay sowing any seed outdoors or setting out plants until after the last frost.

Most seeds will not germinate until the soil warms up to about 60 degrees. If they are sowed in soil cooler than this, they will very likely rot before they germinate. Even if this doesn't happen, they will remain dormant and refuse to sprout until the soil warms up.

You can, however, get a jump on things by starting seeds indoors. But, here again, don't be impatient. Start no sooner than 8 weeks before the average date of the last killing frost in your area. If you start earlier than this, the plants will be too large for satisfactory transplanting by the time the weather is warm enough for them to be set outside.

"Sale"

Go on a Plant Shopping Spree

Perennial plants may often by purchased from your local nursery or garden shop. This lets you see what the blossoms look like and also gives you an opportunity to select exactly the colors you want for your garden.

Look for plants that are dark green and of compact shape. Plants held too long in warm shopping areas very often will not produce vigorous plants. You can detect this by the thin, pale yellow stems and leaves. Avoid purchasing these plants. Even if they are on sale at bargain prices they might not be a good buy.

The backbone of a good perennial garden is nearly always the named varieties, and they are available everywhere in the United States. The main reason they are so useful is because of their predictability. We know their disease resistance, their tolerance for heat and cold and their general habits of height and branching. You can scarcely "go wrong" purchasing one or several of these.

There is plenty of choice. You can select plants of named varieties for special colors or growing habits. And, in time, you can propagate these by cuttings or clump divisions. Colors will come true from such cuttings and divisions. Many perennials will not grow true to type from seed. You may get many off-types as to color, flower form, height, and habit of growth.

Still, you may want to try from time to time, so here's how! You can sow the seeds directly in the beds where the plants are to remain, or you can start them indoors and set them out in beds after the date of the last killing frost in your area.

However, generally speaking, I do not recommend starting seed indoors. Unless you are willing to invest in special lighting equipment and devote considerable time and care, it is usually best to buy plants or to sow the seed directly in the garden. Indoor started plants are seldom as satisfactory for setting out as those bought from nurserymen. And they seldom grow as well or bloom as abundantly as those planted directly in the garden.

Nevertheless, there are exceptions to all rules, and there are many perennials which are best grown from seed each year. Many of these, the so-called biennials — plants that flower the second year — are grown only from seed. These include columbine, foxglove, Canterbury bells, sweet william and delphinium.

Be careful to buy good seed. Be sure your seed is fresh. Many seed packages are now dated, so look for this when you are making your selections. Do not buy too far in advance of planting time.

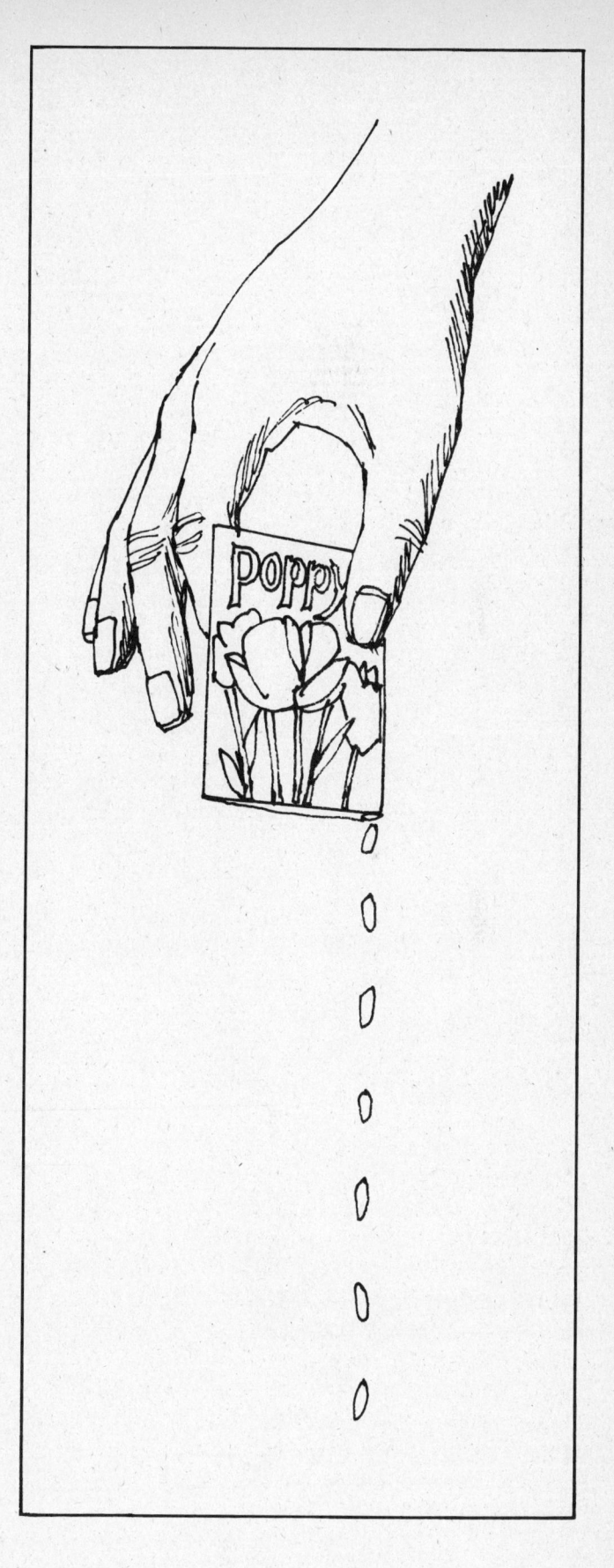

F1 hybrid seeds are a little more expensive than others, but results like this make them worth the price.

Old seed saved from previous years may lose much of its vitality under household conditions. It tends to germinate slowly and to produce poor seedlings. (I have had good luck with keeping seeds from one season to the next in a tightly closed receptacle in my refrigerator. You might try this with partially used packages.)

In any event, keep the seed you have purchased dry and cool until you plant it. Some seed packages have special storage instructions printed on the package. If given, follow these.

When you shop for seeds, look for the new varieties listed as F1 (first generation) hybrids. These have long been available for annuals and are now beginning to show up in perennials also. Such seeds usually cost a little more than the usual inbred varieties, but their superiority makes them worth the extra price.

F1 hybrids are produced by crossing selected inbred parents. These hybrid varieties are more uniform in size and more vigorous than plants of inbred varieties — and they will nearly always produce more flowers.

To sterilize clay pots and wooden flats, swab them with a solution of 1 part chlorine bleach to 10 parts water.

Going to Seed

Getting everything all together is just as important when you plan to start perennial plants from seed as it is when you are doing anything else. Gather your materials, which should consist of wooden or fiber flats, potting strips or peat pots, potting soil (equal parts of garden soil, vermiculite, and sphagnum peat moss or bagged soil mix from garden or variety stores), vermiculite, watering can, polyethlene film for covering, and, of course, seeds.

If you use wooden boxes or clay flower pots for soil containers, clean them well. Soak clay pots in water and scrub them to remove any traces of white fertilizer crust which may remain on the outside.

Sterilize clay pots and boxes by baking them in the oven when you are sterilizing the soil mixture. Or swab the pots and boxes with a solution of one part chlorine bleach to ten parts water. Allow the containers to dry thoroughly, in the sun if possible, before filling them with soil.

There's a good reason for all this hospital-like sanitation. Home-started seedlings are frequently attacked by a fungus disease called damping off. If it occurs, even those seedlings that escape the disease are usually weak and spindly and never become really good garden plants. Conditions of light, temperature, and humidity normally found in our homes are usually unfavorable to plant growth.

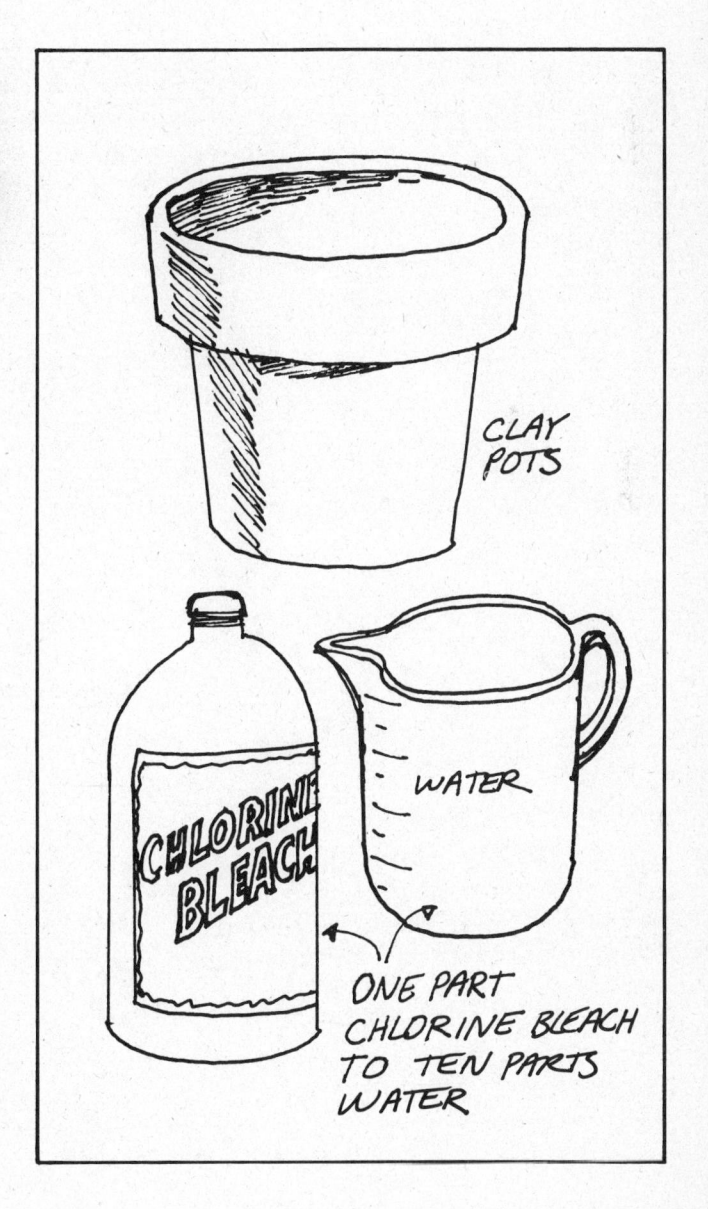

Damping-off organisms cause seeds to rot and seedlings to collapse and die. The disease is carried in soil and may be present on planting containers and tools. Soil moisture and temperature necessary for germination of seeds are also ideal for development of damping-off. Once the disease appears in a seed flat, it may travel quickly through the flat and kill every seedling planted there.

Cheer up. It can be prevented.

Down with Damping Off!

The seeds may be treated with thiram, chloranil, dichlone, or captan — all available at garden centers under various trade names. To treat the seeds tear off the corner of the seed packet and insert about as much fungicide dust as you can pick up on the tip of the small blade of a penknife. Close the hole by folding over the corner of the packet, then shake the seed thoroughly to coat it with the fungicide dust. Place it aside until ready to plant.

Using fiber seed flats or peat pots will help to avoid introducing the damp-off organism. Such containers are usually sterile, inexpensive and available at garden centers. Fiber flats are both light and strong and cost so little that they may be discarded after one use. Peat pots can be set out in the garden along with the plants they contain. Once set in the soil, they will begin to break down and the roots of the plants will grow right through them, feeding upon the material of the pot as it breaks down into soil. Plants grown in peat pots suffer no setback when they are transplanted to the garden. Plants such as larkspur and poppy, which ordinarily do not take kindly to transplanting, can be grown quite satisfactorily in peat pots.

To plant, place two or three large seeds or a "pinch" of small seeds in each pot of soil. Firm the soil with the flat of your hand, or press lightly with an empty pot, being careful not to disturb the seeds. Cover the seeds with fine vermiculite and firm again. Water thoroughly with a mister or fine spray and allow to drain.

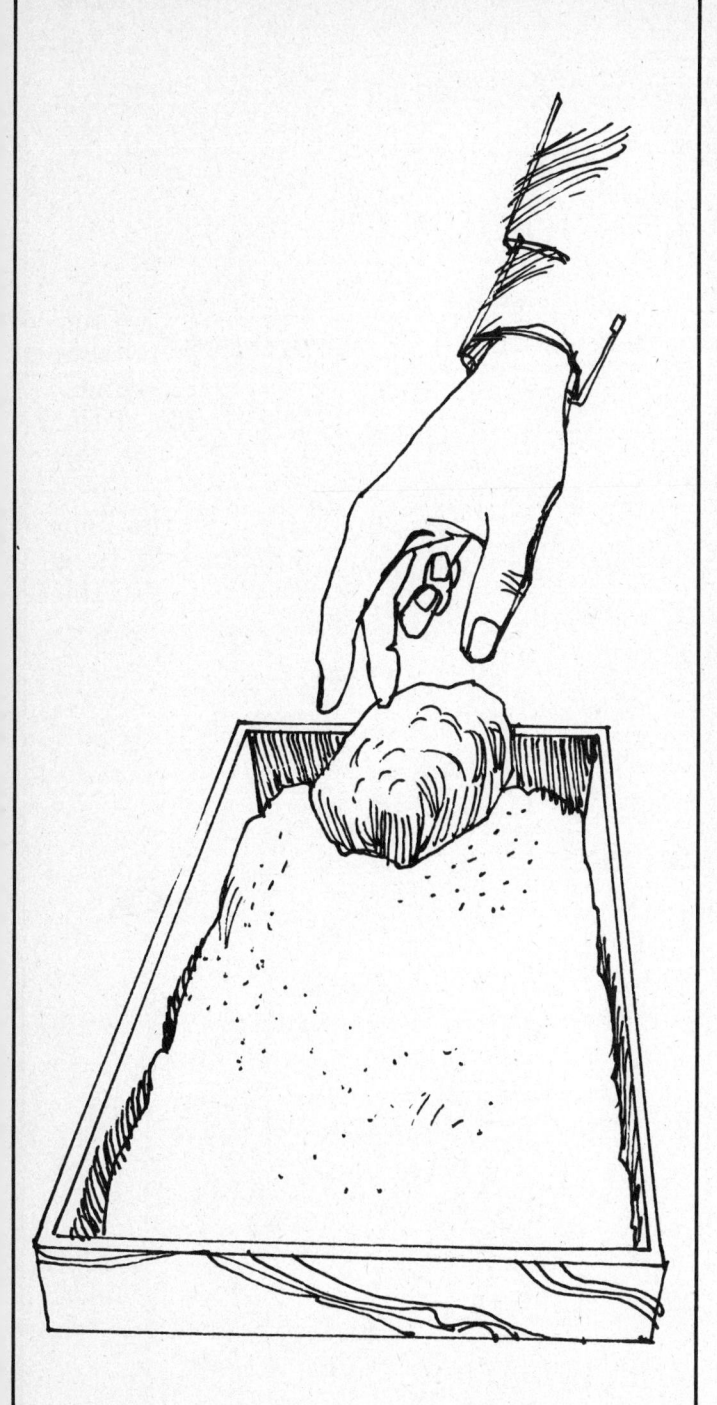

Sterilize the soil in an oven. To do this fill a shallow pan or metal tray with moist but not wet soil. Bury a raw, medium-size potato in the center of the soil. Bake in a medium oven. When the potato is cooked, the soil should also be sterile.

A Fantastic Plastic Cover

Cover the flat with polyethylene film and put it in a warm place (65° to 75°). The flat will need no further watering until after the seeds have germinated. Nor does it need light. Never place the plastic-covered flat in sunlight, as heat build-up under the plastic could kill the emerging seedlings.

Depending on variety, the seeds should germinate in about five days to three weeks. As soon as they poke their perky little pointed heads through the vermiculite, remove the plastic covering. Don't give them full light at once; move them to a lightly shaded area first.

As they grow, give them more light, but protect them during bright weather with a light shade. The trays may be covered with a single layer of cheese cloth, inexpensive muslin, or part of an old sheet. Construct a simple frame to support the shading material. If you make it of wire, attach the shade material to the frame with shower-curtain rings so that it can be closed on bright days and opened on cloudy ones.

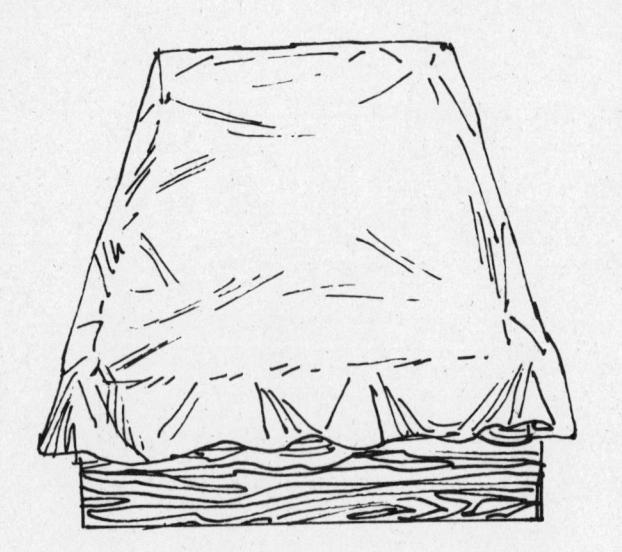

A Solution for Famished Flowers

Water and fertilize the new plants frequently. Like growing children, they need plenty of each—and they need it oftener. Make it easy on yourself by doing both of these jobs at once, using a solution of one tablespoon of soluble fertilizer (20-20-20) in a gallon of water. Thoroughly moisten the soil, but be careful not to wash out the small seedlings. If possible, apply the solution as a fine mist. If you don't happen to have a mister, place the solution in a container a bit larger than the pots and submerge them up to their rims. The soil in the pots will soak up the solution from the bottom. Remove the pots as soon as the soil is completely moistened. Allow any excess to drain off.

Time to Move On

Most gardeners think of transplanting seedlings in the spring of the year. For the most part, this is quite logical, for less-hardy, late-flowering types and those having evergreen foliage often make the best growth if started early and transplanted in spring. Perennials included in this group are bee balm, Shasta daisy and chrysanthemum.

But there are also many perennials which take kindly to transplanting at midsummer and even early fall. This should always be done well in advance of cold weather so they will have a chance to become established before winter. The summer warmth retained in the soil promotes good root growth so by spring the plants are well on their way with their little systems in good order. This helps them to better withstand any hot, dry weather they may be subjected to the following summer.

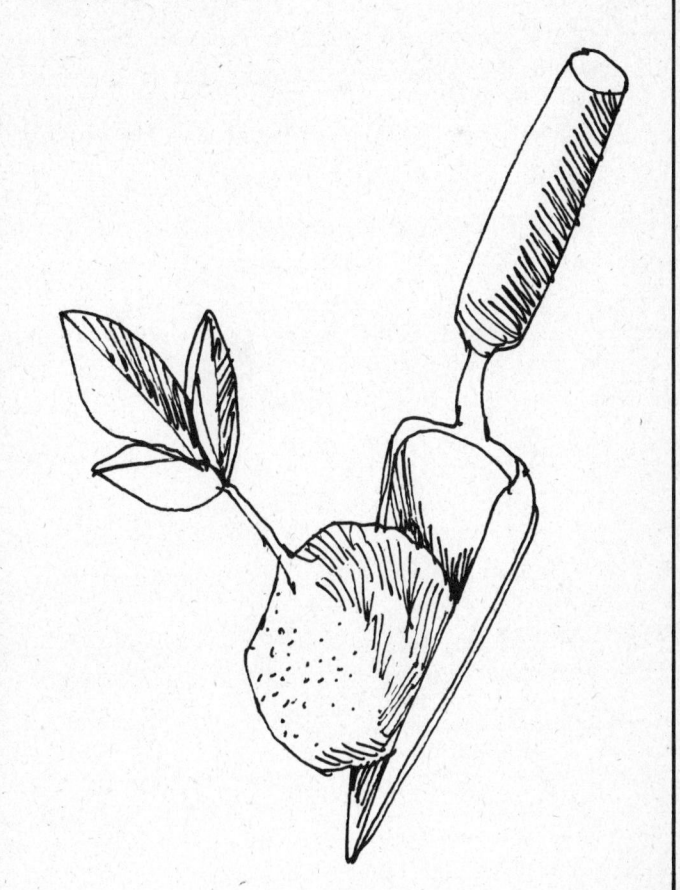

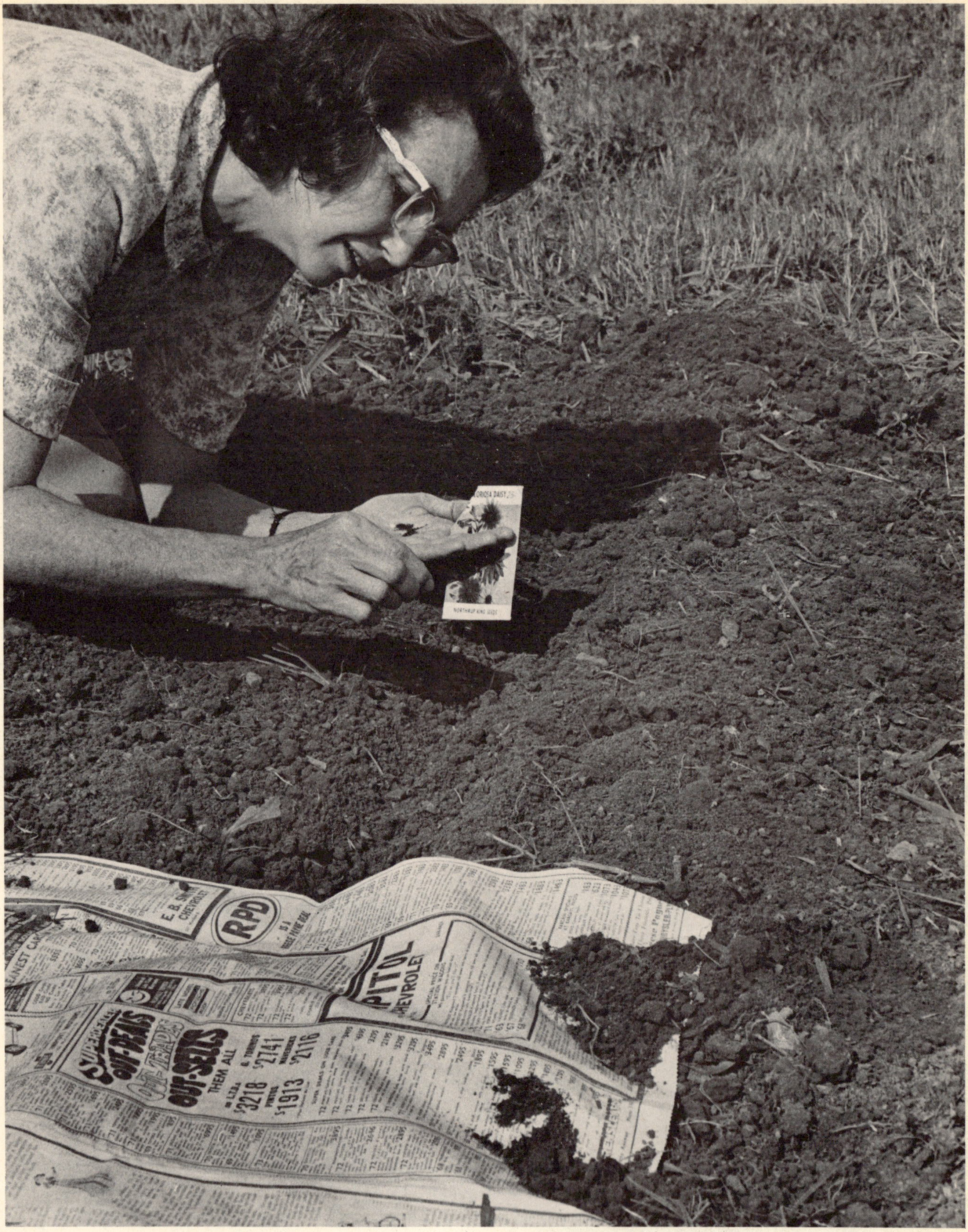
RPD
CHEVROLET
OUT-SELLS
THEM ALL

Covering newly planted seeds with newspaper or plastic keeps the soil from drying out.

Don't Be Foiled by Bad Soil

Perennials seeded directly in the garden may fail to germinate properly because of the condition of the soil. This happens most frequently when the surface cakes and thus prevents the entry of water. You can avoid this by sowing the seed in vermiculite-filled furrows. Make the furrows about half an inch deep, fill them with fine vermiculite, and sprinkle with water. Then make another shallow furrow in the medium and sow the seed in the furrow. Check the rate recommended on the packet. Cover the seed with a layer of vermiculite, again following the recommended depth for sowing. Spray with a mister or adjust your hose nozzle to a fine mist and water the seeded area thoroughly.

You can retard water evaporation by covering the seeded area with sheets of newspaper or polyethylene film. Used plastic garment bags from the dry cleaner are also excellent. Support the newspaper or plastic so it will be raised an inch or two above the surface of the bed. Remove when seedlings appear. Cardboard boxes are also handy for placing over the seedbed, especially if you live in a windy section. Weight them down with a brick or stone.

As soon as your outdoor-grown perennials develop two true leaves, they should be thinned to the recommended spacing. Don't delay. Thinning permits them to have enough light, water and nutrients to develop fully; crowding causes them to grow tall and spindly. If your plants have sprouted in vermiculite-filled furrows, it is easy to transplant the extra seedlings to another spot without injury.

Perennials grown in peat pots and flats are healthy and eager to go to work in your garden.

The Kindest Cut of All

Plants purchased from a nursery or started indoors should both be set out in the same way. When the right time arrives, remove them from the flat by slicing downward into the soil between the plants. Try to lift out each plant with a block of soil surrounding its roots and set the soil block in the planting hole.

If the plants are in fiber pots, remove the paper from the outside of the root mass and set the plant in a prepared planting hole.

If plants are in peat pots, remove the top edge of the pot so that rainwater will not collect around the plant. The pot, as well as its contents, should be thoroughly moistened to help the roots develop properly. The soil around the planting hole should be thoroughly drenched with a liquid fertilizer like 16-52-10 or 20-20-20 . Mix one tablespoon into a gallon of water and water thoroughly. Place the moistened pot in the planting hole, pressing the soil up around it. The root growth and moisture will, in a short time, cause the pot to break down in the soil, and the soil around the plant will be improved.

A PANSY TREE

Even if you have no room for a flower bed, you can enjoy the bright, smiling faces of pansies. With a little effort, you can create a pansy tree on your balcony or patio, or you can hang a cylinder of pansies outside your window.

To build a tree, wrap a cylinder of chicken wire around a broad board. Staple or nail it to the narrow edges of the board, leaving plenty of space between the broad sides of the board and the wire. Line the wire with sphagnum moss, then fill the cylinder with a lightweight commercial planting mix or with a mixture of 70 percent peat moss and 30 percent perlite.

For a small hanging planter, find an empty can the same diameter as you want your cylinder to be. With a pair of tin snips, cut around the sides of the can about 2 inches above the bottom. Staple a cylinder of chicken wire over the slats, then fill it with sphagnum moss and soil mix. Drill holes in the slats and run a wire through them for hanging.

Be very careful when planting your cylindrical gardens. Try not to damage the young plants' roots as you insert them through the chicken wire. After planting, water thoroughly. If possible, keep the planter out of direct sun and wind for about a week. At the end of this first week, feed the plants with a complete liquid fertilizer. From then on, feed the plants once a week and water frequently. Planters of this type dry out very rapidly.

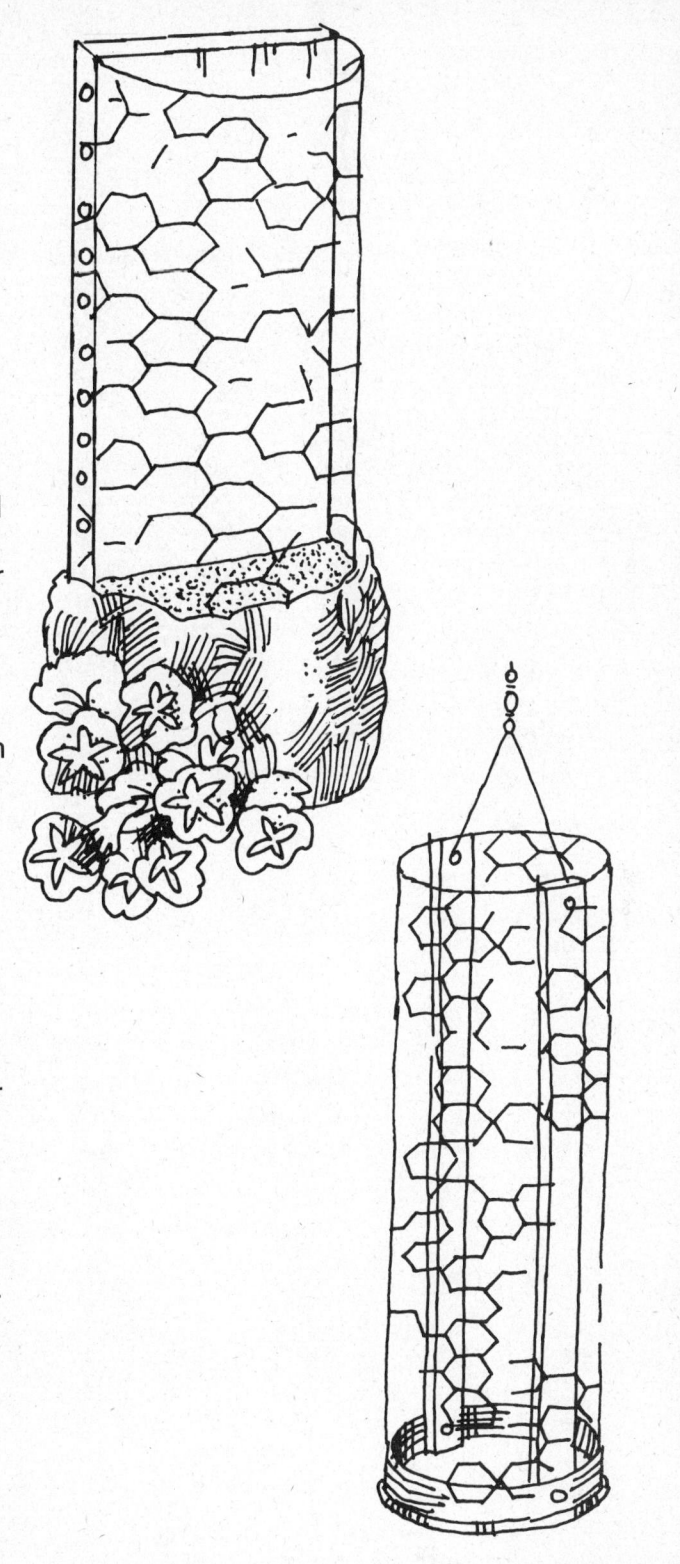

Irises are tough and hardy and will grow almost anywhere.

Bare-Root Cuttings Bear Up Well

Irises are very durable perennials. I have had them lie around all summer outdoors, exposed to sun and wind, and still grow when they were planted. I do not recommend this, but it is a good illustration of how wonderfully strong and viable this particular perennial is. It is always, so far as I know, sold as a bare root and no particular care is necessary, other than getting it into the ground as soon as possible so it will start to produce those deceptively delicate-looking flowers that the French call "fleur-de-lis." I always think of these fellows, especially the tall bearded ones, as the sentinels of the garden, standing straight and tall overseeing the smaller plants and generally keeping order.

Peonies are another perennial sold in bare root divisions, usually with three or five "eyes." When a peony root is divided, each piece of root that has a bud attached to it will grow and produce another plant just like the parent. Peonies are exceedingly beautiful, but don't get carried away, for they are large plants and will occupy considerable space after they are through blooming. They are fine for planting in open spaces between shrubs or for naturalizing in a woodland.

September is generally considered the ideal planting time for peonies; but early spring will be all right if the ground is in good condition. Place the plants so that the crowns, or tops, are covered with about 2 inches of soil. In a good location and with proper care, herbaceous peonies will continue to blossom satisfactorily for a long time, possibly twenty years or more, so consider well the location you put them in for they don't like to be moved around.

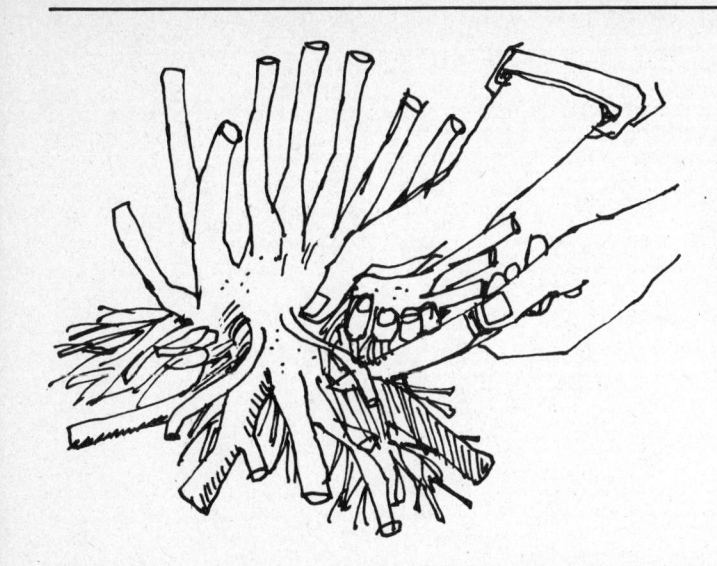

Digging

To divide peonies, dig up the entire plant and shake the soil away from the roots. Cut the plant into divisions, each with 3 to 5 eyes.

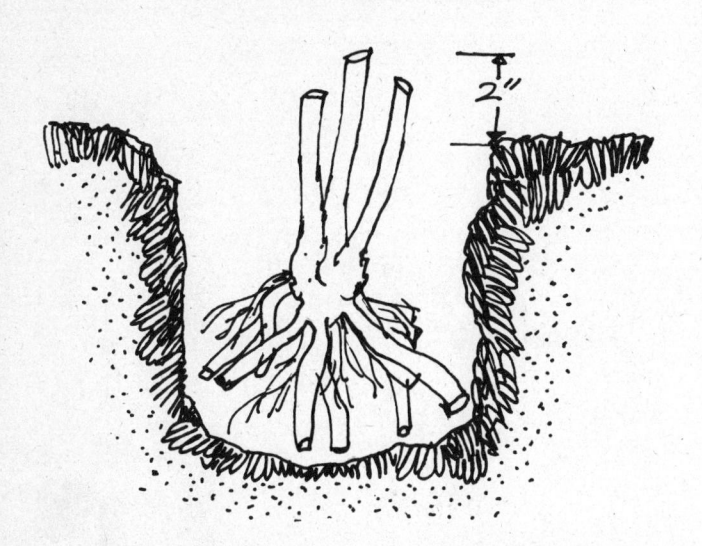

Planting

Before planting the divisions, thoroughly tamp down the soil in the planting hole. Set the division in the hole, making sure that no eye is more than 2 inches below the surface, and cover.

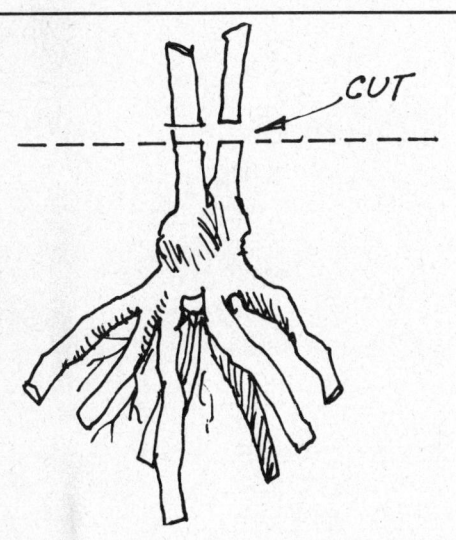

Cutting Off

Firm the soil to eliminate air pockets. Cut off any stubs that are above the ground to help prevent an attack of botrytis.

The following chart should help you keep your garden well-groomed and well-bloomed throughout the growing season. Asterisks indicate plants which will tolerate shade.

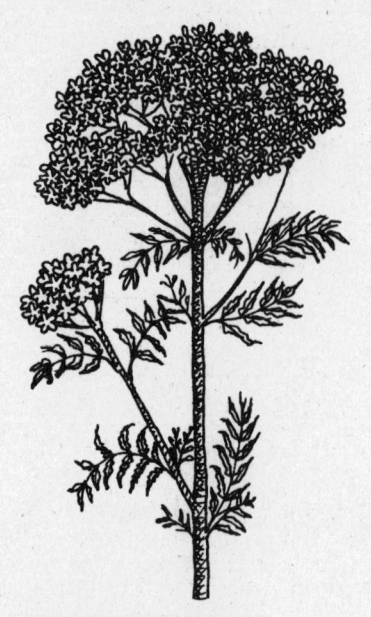

EARLY SPRING

Sweet William	15"
Candytuft	9"
Pinks	8"
Creeping Phlox	6"
*Bleeding Heart	18"
*Violets	8"
Primrose	12"

LATE SPRING

*Astilbe	18"
Carnation	12"
*Columbine	18"
Gaillardia	15"
*Forget-Me-Not	10"
Pyrethrum	15"
Peony	36"
Poppy	24"
Iris	24"
Shasta Daisy	24"

SUMMER

Day lily	30"
*Foxglove	36"
Delphinium	36"
Baby's Breath	30"
Hollyhocks	72"
Heliotrope	12"
Lavender	18"
Platycodon	24"

FALL

Asters	24"
Helianthus	48"
Lythrum	24"
Chrysanthemems	24"

Beds

That tiny plant you bought may become as large as the one below in a few years, so give it plenty of elbow room.

If you are an average gardener and can spare only a few hours each week to work in your garden, you probably feel that this time must count for the utmost in achievement. So, before you drop in at the local garden center or nursery, look over the area you plan to landscape thoroughly, very thoroughly. Plan your garden, beds or borders on paper first. A rough drawing will do — you don't need to call in a landscape architect. And be very conservative — remember that that tiny little plant can spread out amazingly in a year or so, occupying all its own space and maybe sneaking a little more from somebody else.

Consider all the other permanent features, such as outbuildings, the garage, walls, walks, fences, service yards. Some of these may be enhanced by perennials planted in front of or alongside them. You may wish to partially screen others.

If you plan to do most of the gardening chores yourself, you will want the beds arranged conveniently. Don't make them too wide. Six to eight feet will allow for a wide choice of plants, some to bloom early, others in midseason, and still others late. Arrange matters so you can have a continuous display of color.

Since most of the tall perennials flower in late summer or early fall, they should form the back of the border, with the smaller ones placed toward the front. Don't exclude the tall plants from the middle — a few placed here and there will help you to avoid monotony and make for a more interesting planting. "Tall" plants are those which usually attain a height of three feet or more at maturity.

The middle row, conssiting of more plants that range in height from 2 to 3 feet, will mostly be composed of the midsummer-flowering group. The shortest plants, the spring-flowering-ones which grow 2 feet tall on the average, will make up the front row.

45

Moving Pictures

I think curved-line plantings are far more graceful and interesting than long, straight beds. Open areas of lawn add interest by contrast. Make the rough sketch fairly large. You can open up a big, brown paper sack if you have nothing else. Then use something to help you envision what the border will look like when it is planted. An old nursery or seed catalog that shows the various perennials you have in mind may be of help. Cut out the pictures, and place them on your diagram.

Move the pictures around until you feel they are pleasingly placed. They will be much easier to move at this time than after the real McCoys have been planted and you decide they should have gone somewhere else. As you clip the pictures, jot down the information on each one — height, color, time of bloom and growth habits.

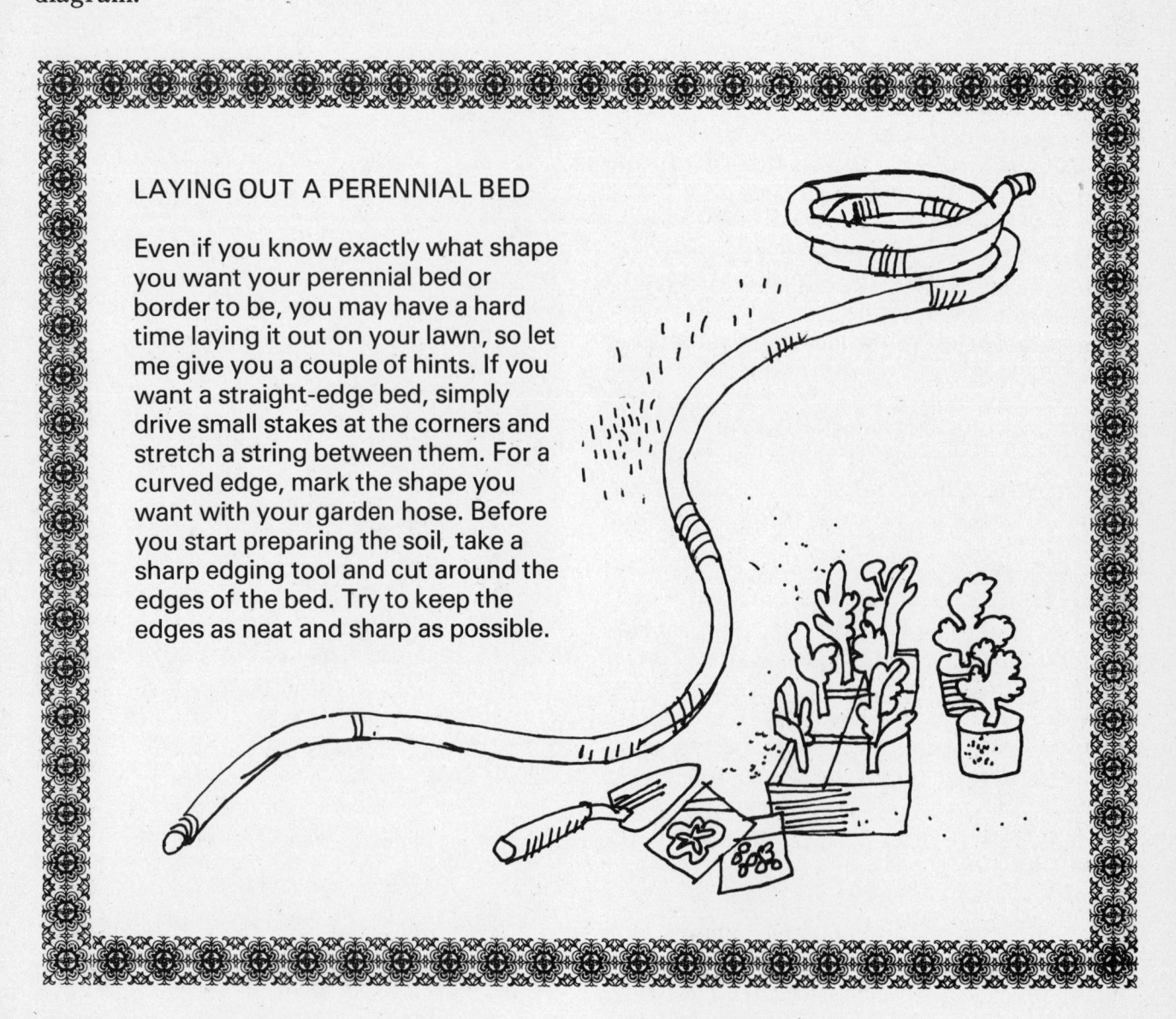

LAYING OUT A PERENNIAL BED

Even if you know exactly what shape you want your perennial bed or border to be, you may have a hard time laying it out on your lawn, so let me give you a couple of hints. If you want a straight-edge bed, simply drive small stakes at the corners and stretch a string between them. For a curved edge, mark the shape you want with your garden hose. Before you start preparing the soil, take a sharp edging tool and cut around the edges of the bed. Try to keep the edges as neat and sharp as possible.

Thrift is an exceptionally fine border plant.

Having arrived at some conclusion, you can work toward your goal. Stagger your purchases over a period of time — even a year or two if need be. While you are waiting to buy the more expensive plants, fill in with bulbs and annuals.

Down through the ages gardeners have used various means to retain a line of demarcation between lawn and flower beds, using stone, brick and wood. The best answer I have found to this problem is a metal strip set flush with the grade. It is neat, unobtrusive and out of the way.

Hold That Line!

For curved beds, I like the looks of living edges. I have already mentioned the obliging qualities of day lilies whose flexible, arching foliage is easy to mow under. Another good edging is liriope, sometimes called lily-turf, an evergreen perennial which grows easily in full sun or deep shade and is not particular about soil requirements.

Liriope has flowers similar to grape hyacinth, but larger. These are borne abundantly in late summer and are followed by polished black berries. Mature plants grow about 1 foot tall and have a spread of about a foot. Liriope is propagated by division of the clumps immediately after flowering.

Perennial candytuft, which grows only about a foot tall when in bloom, is another excellent choice. As soon as the blooms fade, it can be cut down to a 6-inch height. While full sun is preferable, it will also grow reasonably well in half shade.

The lovely herbaceous perennial, thrift or sea pink (Armeria maritima), is exceptionally valuable for edging use, especially in sandy soils. As it is evergreen, it looks well at all seasons. The foliage is delicate and grasslike in texture, and the deep rose pink flower heads are borne on 6-inch stalks in the spring.

Plant Perennials Pronto!

As with all planting, the watchword is "Don't delay!" Probably more plants have given up their lives because of delayed planting than to all the insects and diseases put together. Plants that must come through the mails, no matter how carefully wrapped, have two strikes against them already, due to the vagaries of mail delivery and the possibility of having been sat upon by other, heavier packages during their journey, not to mention being kept in close, warm room, for many hours. Get them into the ground without delay. Do this also when a local nursery delivers, or when you go shopping and bring them home yourself. Don't let them languish in the back of the car, tired and thirsty.

The wrappings differ greatly, some being individually clothed in paper and moss, and others loose and bare-rooted.

Plant the individually wrapped plants first, consulting your garden plan as you go so each will enter its new home at the right time and don't expose them to drying winds at any time. A coudy, humid day is always best for planting. If you're purchasing from a local nursery, this is something good to remember.

For most perennials you should dig a hole a little wider than the plant and only as deep as it stood in the nursery. The rhizome-rooted plants, such as irises, should be planted with the roots below the surface of the ground and the rhizome just on the surface. To do this effectively, dig a hole wide enough to accomodate the long rhizome and then build up a little mound in the center. Set the rhizome on this so it will be about even with the surface of the surrounding bed. Let the roots hang downward, cover with soil, packing carefully so all are covered. The rhizome of an iris must feel the kiss of the warm sun or it will not bloom well.

Plants on which the leaves spring from a central crown should be planted with this crown just at the dirt line—much as you plant strawberries.

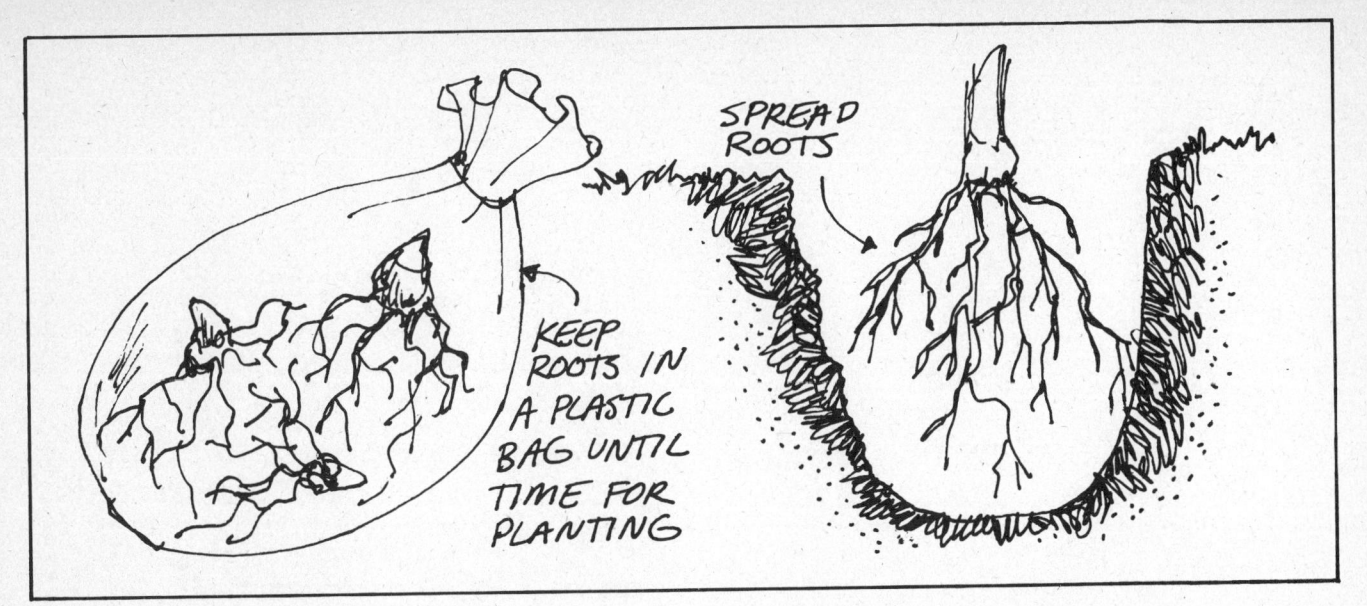

A Home for Hilda Hollyhock

Still another group of perennials, those with fleshy roots, such as Oriental poppies or hollyhocks, should be planted with the tap root running straight down and the bud just below the surface of the soil. Always be careful in all planting to have the hole large enough so the roots can spread out naturally without crowding. Soil should be brought in contact with all the roots and firmly pressed down. Always water thoroughly when planting is completed.

Any broken or mangled roots of the fleshy-rooted types should be trimmed off with a sharp knife. Cut back to healthy, sound tissue.

Try to prevent roots from drying out at all times. Keep them covered as much as possible. Carrying them about with you in a large plastic bag is convenient. Try to work quickly.

Roots that become bunched together by packing should be loosened and spread out as you plant. Again, remember to make the hole large enough to prevent crowding.

Most perennials should not be set any deeper than they were previously growing in the nursery. This will usually be easy to determine by looking at the stem of the plant. The portion above the soil line will be lighter in color.

As you cover the roots with soil, don't just shovel it in willy-nilly. Crumble it with your hands and work it among and over the roots, firming it as you go. Bringing the moist soil in contact with the roots will eliminate air pockets, as does watering when the planting is completed. Firming the soil also helps to keep the plant steady, and it keeps it from heaving due to alternate freezing and thawing during the winter.

Try not to plant when the soil is wet and cloddy. Such times are hard on both you and the plants. It is difficult to work the soil and watering to settle the plant in may do more harm than good.

When planting fleshy-rooted perennials, carry them to the garden in a plastic bag to keep them from drying out. Also remember to spread the roots evenly in the planting hole.

Care

Cultivation of perennials should always be done with a light hand, digging only into the top inch or so of the soil with your hoe or scratcher to remove any young weeds. Of course, weeding must be done occasionally, but always remember that these plants are shallow-rooted and deep cultivation is likely to injure them. Mulching to prevent weeds growth is always preferable to cultivation.

How Much Mulch?

There are no hard and fast rules for the depth of a mulch. Much depends on the type of soil and the material of the mulch itself. A soil that is largely composed of sand and gravel will need more mulching than a heavy clay soil. Do a little testing. And think about the service you want the mulch to perform. It should be deep enough to kill the weeds and prevent the soil from drying out, but it must not be so deep that it prevents air and rainwater from reaching the soil.

To be most effective the mulch should be applied well in advance of the time that weeds start into active growth and while there is still some moisture in the soil from the spring rains.

Any organic material may be used as a mulch. Ideally, it should decompose readily, be free of elements harmful to plants, and be free of weed seeds. Materials often used are old straw, hay, well-rotted manure, composted leaves, grass clippings, sawdust, pine needles, buckwheat hulls, cocoa shells, coffee grounds, ground corncobs, peanut shells, peat moss, salt hay, wood chips and wood shavings. If you can obtain nothing else, you can even use paper, polyethylene film or aluminum foil.

Spread the mulching material in an even layer around and under plants to a depth of several inches. Loose, coarse material will settle down to about half of its original depth.

Whenever possible, apply mulching material after a light rain or irrigation. Do not, however, mulch heavy, wet soils that are poorly drained. Try to use partially decomposed materials instead of fresh ones to prevent losses of moisture and nitrogen.

If hay or straw is used to mulch, presprout any harmful weed or grass seed that may be present. This may be done by sprinkling or soaking the material with water for a period of two or three weeks.

Sawdust, wood chips and wood shavings are all good materials to use for mulching. However, nitrogen in some form should be added to overcome the effect of these materials on the soil. Add about ½ pound of ammonium nitrate, or its equivalent, to each bushel of sawdust. A one-inch layer of sawdust is adequate for shallow-rooted plants; a slightly heavier application should be given to the deeper-rooted ones. Apply before the plants get too large, and be sure to spread under and around the plants as well as in the middle of the row.

Mulches, especially grass clippings and compost, add organic matter to the soil and furnish food for earthworms, which are valuable in aerating the soil. The organic matter helps to keep the soil crumbly and easy to work, or in "good tilth".

Raindrops Keep Falling on My Bed

It is a mistake to rely on summer rainfall to keep your flower beds watered. All too often it will not come at the right time. Plan to irrigate your perennials from the beginning. Correct watering, at the right time and in the right amount, can make the difference between a good flower display and a disappointing one.

If natural rainfall is insufficient, plan to water on a regular schedule. Perennials should be watered during the entire growing season, particularly during hot, dry weather.

When you water, the entire bed should be thoroughly moistened, but do not water so heavily that the soil becomes soggy. Check from time to time, and water again when the soil feels dry to the touch. Also watch the plants—if the tips wilt slightly at midday it is time to water again.

A canvas soaker hose is fine for watering beds. Water from a soaker hose seeps

"Nothing's worrying me!"

When rainfall is scanty, produce your own

directly into the soil without waste and without disturbing the soil surfaces.

If you water with a sprinkler, use an oscillating type. This will cover a large area and produce rain-like drops of water. I do not like the rotating type. They tend to tear up the surface of the soil, and they cover a relatively small area.

Feeding

All through this book, or for that matter, just about any gardening book you pick up, you are confronted from time to time with suggestions that you use something referred to as 5-10-5 or 10-20-10. It's kind of frustrating if you can't figure out what the heck they're talking about. Well, it's really pretty simple because all this is is a fertilizer formula expressed in numbers. The three figures, usually separated by dashes, indicate the proportions in which plant nutrients are present. The first number is the proportion of nitrogen, the second phosphorus, and the third potassium.

As an example, a 10-20-10 fertilizer contains twice as much of each nutrient as does a 5-10-5 fertilizer. The proportions, however, are identical. You would need to apply just half as much of the 10-20-10 fertilizer as you would of the 5-10-5 fertilizer. The advantage of the 10-20-10 is that it is lighter, and less bulky so it requires less storage space. On the other hand, the 5-10-5 may be less expensive.

A fertilizer which analyzes 5-10-10 will be proportionately much richer in potash than a 5-10-5 or a 10-20-10 and more useful if root stimulation is desirable. A fertilizer richer in nitrogen and phosphorus such as 6-10-4, is what you need to produce heavy foliage growth. If increased flower production is the end result you're seeking, a low-nitrogen fertilizer such as 0-10-5 or 2-10-5 would be the better choice.

53

Tall, single-stemmed perennials should be staked with a cane three-fourths as tall as a mature plant. Loop soft twine loosely around the stem, and tie it tightly to the stake.

A circle of wire mounted on 3 legs is best for supporting large, bushy clumps of perennials. Be sure to sink the legs 6 to 8 inches into the ground.

Fences Make Good Neighbors

If your perennial bed is near a wall or fence, you can use it to support top-heavy plants. How to do it is something else again — you don't want your plants to look as if they are being choked to death.

If the wall is a solid one, masonry or brick, you may use tightly stretched wires set a couple of feet apart on brackets. Allow them to extend several inches from the wall. A good-looking wooden trellis may also be employed for this purpose.

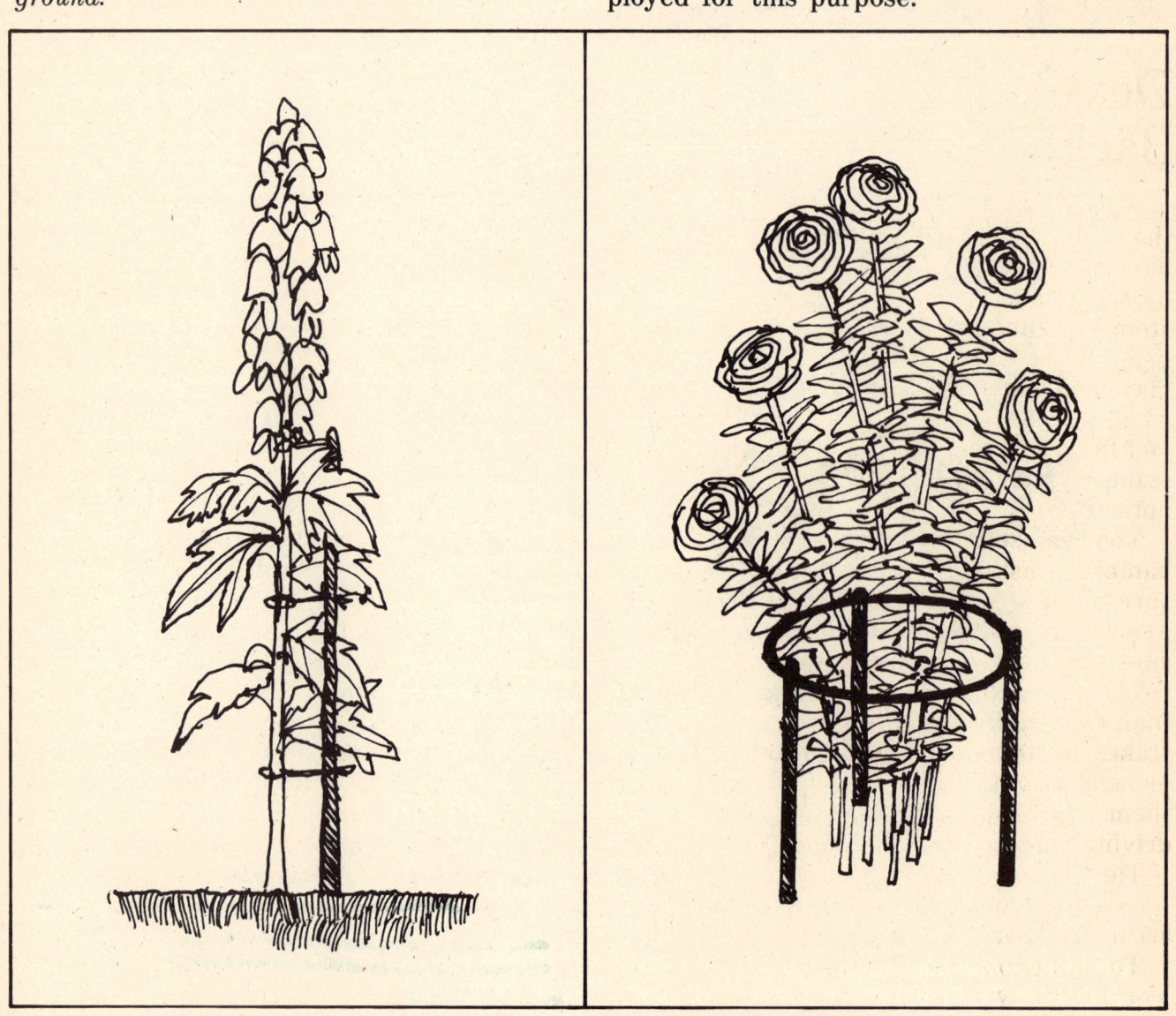

Peonies are often supported by means of a hoop on a tripod. This is put over the plant at the time they are in bud, before the heavy flower heads develop and cause the stems to bend under their weight. Those sold in garden centers are usually of metal. If you don't like the looks of these, you can wrap them with green florist's tape. Or you can make your own rings out of flexible branches, such as those of willow. Tie several shoots of the right length together, cover them with the florist's tape, and put them on stakes or forked sticks at the right height to support the peonies.

Avoid a floppy look to your flower beds by lifting the flowers with a wire or wooden support.

Developing Backbone

Almost all perennials are top-heavy. If they are not staked or provided some other means of support, a heavy toll will be taken by winds and rains. If plants fall over, the stem will function poorly where it has been bent. If the stem is cracked, rot organisms may penetrate the break. To prevent these small garden tragedies, stake plants when you first set them out. The plants cover the stakes as they grow, so they will scarcely be noticeable.

You can use stakes made of wood, dowels, bamboo, plastic or wire. If made of wire, be sure to put a loop on the end so no one will get an eye put out when he bends over to smell the daisies.

The stakes should be 6 to 12 inches shorter than the height of a mature plant. Place the stakes behind the plants, sinking them far enough into the ground to firmly anchor them. They must be able to withstand hard, driving rain and wind.

Tie the plants loosely with wire covered with a layer of paper or plastic. These wires are better than string which rots quickly.

To tie the plant effectively, make a double loop in the wire with one loop around the plant and the other around the stake. Never loop the wire around both stake and plant — the plant will hang to one side, and the wire may girdle the stem.

So that you will have plenty of stakes on hand for your perennials, save appropriate material at shrub-pruning time. Prunings from privet, water sprouts from fruit trees and other similar material are all excellent — and free. Lengths of bamboo cane may also be used. Let any green or partially green stakes dry out for a time before using, or you may find an unwanted tree growing beside your perennial!

A Borderline Case

A perennial border needs careful watching, particularly if grass grows up to the very edge of it. The plants in the front row may reach out and smother the grass or flop over and make it hard to mow. If you grow several different plants in the front row, handling this problem becomes even more difficult. Do yourself a favor. Plan to use a uniform edging plant—there are many suitable for a flower border. Boxwood has long been a favorite for this.

Dwarf heath, lavender and lavender cotton (Santolina) also make attractive edgings. Thrift is very neat and will last for years. Mauve catmint is another charming border plant. The gray-green foliage is mint-scented, and small lavender flowers cover the plant from late spring until midsummer.

That old favorite, moss phlox, makes an interesting edging but must be trimmed as soon as the blossoms have faded so that it will not become straggly and untidy. English ivy is useful as an edging, but the trailing shoots must be clipped and pegged down regularly if you want to keep this eager beaver in bounds.

Arranging beds so they border on a brick, gravel or flagstone walk will also help to keep edgings neat. If you have extensive beds, you might like to purchase an edger-trimmer to cut down on hand trimming.

A Pinch in Time

Should you pinch perennials back if they didn't pinch you first? Absolutely! Pinching back simply involves removing the terminal shoot by pinching with the thumbnail and finger. The purpose is to make the plant shorter and bushier.

Pinching back is particularly important in growing chrysanthemums. When small-flowered varieties are 6 to 8 inches high, pinch off the light green, growing tips to encourage branching. Unless the growing tips are pinched, plants will develop tall, weak stems that produce only a few flowers. After you've pinched them, new branches will develop along the stem. Pinch all shoots every 2 weeks until June 10 for early varieties, until July 1 for late varieties. Flowers will not form if you continue to pinch later than these dates.

Thinning should be practiced with many plants, such as phlox, after new shoots are well started. Remove the weakest plants, allowing more room for the sturdier plants to develop. Thinning and removal of surplus plants should always take place as soon as the best-growing plants become apparent. Crowded plants never develop to their fullest potential.

Thinning does not necessarily mean pulling them out by the roots. If the plants are very thick, pulling may disturb the roots of those you wish to retain. A far better method is to snip the stems off close to the ground when the plants are around 4 to 6 inches tall. The remaining plants will grow more vigorously, and their foliage will soon fill the gaps left by thinning. The flower clusters will also be much larger.

Delphiniums and lupines will bloom in fall as well as spring if you remove the spring flowers when they fade.

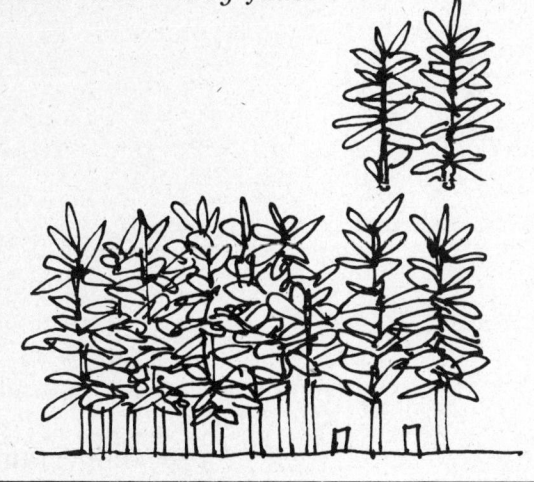

When the new stalks are 6 inches tall, cut the old ones to the ground.

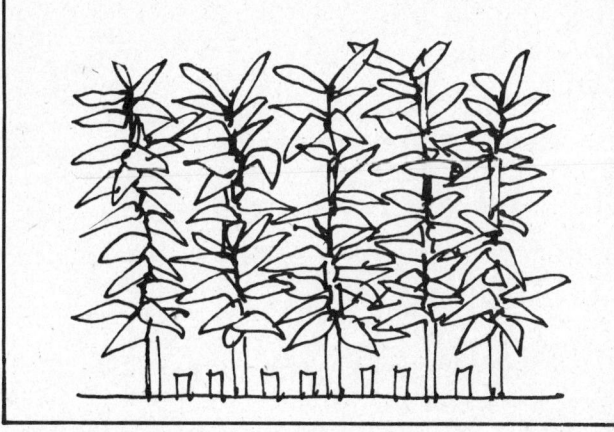

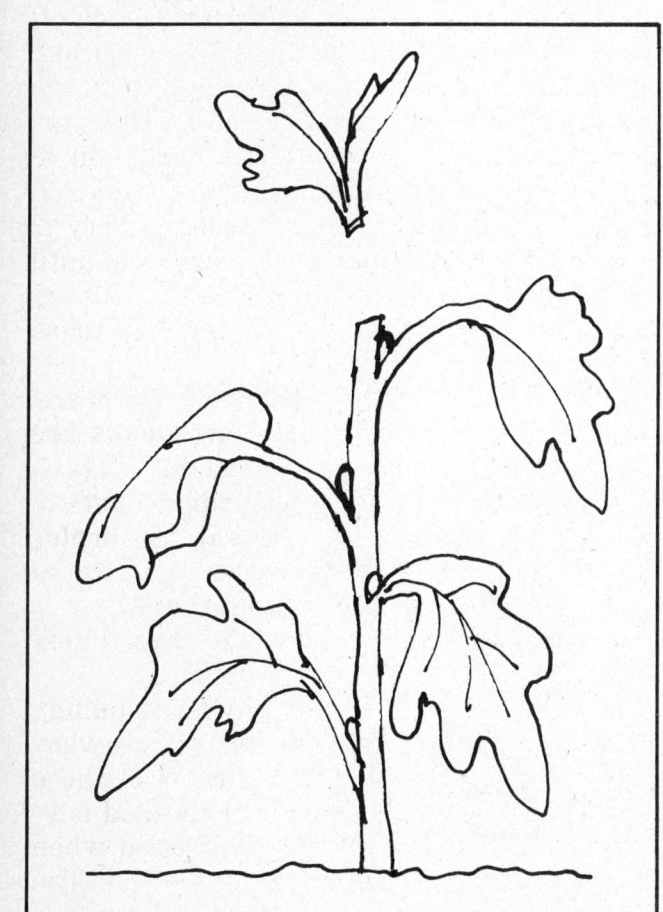

To encourage fall-blooming perennials to bloom profusely, pinch off the tip of each stem when the plants are about 6" tall.

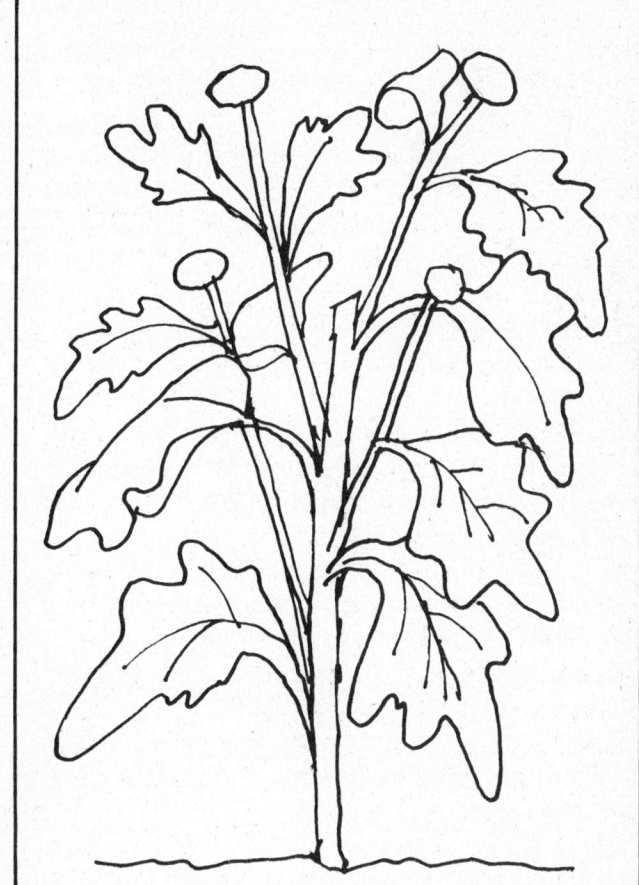

Keep pinching back new shoots until midsummer.

For enormous chrysanthemum or peony blossoms, remove all but the large top bud.

Quality— Not Quantity

If you would like show-sized peony or chrysanthemum blossoms, concentrate growth in a few flowers by taking off the side buds as close to the stem as possible. Only the large top bud should be left. This process, called "disbudding," forces all the strength and energy of the plant into the development of the remaining flower. The single remaining blossom will very likely be a giant — so stand back.

For the large-flowered mums, wait until the plants are 5 to 6 inches high, then pinch out the growing tip. New shoots will develop along the stem. Break off all but 2 or 3 of these new shoots, and let those remaining grow into branches. Every 2 weeks remove all side shoots that grow from these branches. When flower buds show, remove all except those on the top 3 inches of each branch. As these top buds develop, keep an eye on the first, or crown bud. When you are sure it is healthy and well developed, pinch off all the other buds. The stem of the bud should snap off easily at the point where it joins the branch. If the terminal flower bud is injured or looks as if it will not develop, pinch it off and leave the second flower bud from the tip. Continue to remove side branches until flowering time.

This disbudding practice works best with large-flowered species. Disbudding small-flowered varieties will not make them produce large flowers.

Faded Beauties and Seedy Characters

Remove faded blossoms to keep your plants from becoming seedy.

Faded flowers should always be removed as soon as you can conveniently do so. Of course, the most obvious reason for doing so is to keep your plant and your garden looking neat and well-groomed. Less apparent, but equally important, is another reason — to prevent seed from forming. This will not only prevent unwanted offspring, but will also help to conserve the energy of the plant. Prompt removal often encourages the production of a second crop of flowers.

Mama Nature intends for fading flowers to "go to seed" in order to propagate the species. If her first attempt is foiled by you and your pruning shears, she'll convince the plant to try again. It will work hard to bear new flowers so that seed may be produced.

With this procedure, timing really counts. Cut the blossoms after they have faded but before any seed is produced.

The method used and the correct timing vary from plant to plant. With coreopsis, for instance, you should snip off only about the top third of the plant. This will encourage the development of side branches and in time, new flowers. For delphiniums and lupines, cut the stalks just below the faded flowers, leaving as much foliage as you can. Within a short time new shoots will come up from the ground. Now, as the old stalks wither and the leaves begin to dry and turn brown, remove the entire old stalk. If you cut old stalks before new shoots appear, you may cause the entire plant to die.

Some plants may not flower a second time. Even so, it is better to remove faded flowers. This allows the plant to conserve its energies and build a strong root system for the following year, rather than waste its strength making seed.

"Chrysanthemum dead-ahead, squadron!"

Pests

Perennials, though usually remarkably healthy, are not immune to insect infestations. If you allow your insect enemies to get a foothold in the perennial bed, they can seriously damage or even destroy your prized plants. Iris borers, for example, munch their way down through the soft, inner tissues of the leaves and end up in the roots. These insidious insects not only weaken the plants with their chewing, they frequently infect it with soft rot.

Keeping your garden clean will go a long way toward preventing serious problems. Remove all weeds and dead plants which might harbor pests.

Check your plants for insects regularly. The chart below should help you identify some of your enemies. If you see a few insects, pick them off by hand and drop them into a can of kerosene or knock them off with a hard jet of water. If you take care of the problem at this early stage, you may not have to resort to more severe measures.

Sometimes, however, you may have to use some of the chemical controls listed below.

APHIDS

Aphids, or plant lice, are small sucking insects yellowish-green to black in color. They feed on new shoots, flower buds, and roots, causing the plant to become stunted and deformed. Aphids also secrete a sticky substance in which sooty mold, a fungus, thrives.

A hard jet of water will usually dislodge most aphids. If this does not work spray with malathion or dimethoate.

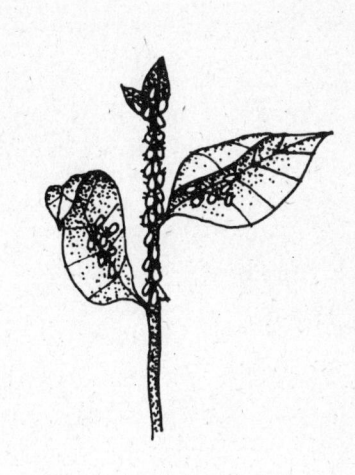

IRIS BORERS

Iris borers are the larvae of moths which lay their eggs in dead iris stalks and other garden debris in the fall. In spring, when the borers hatch, they bore into new iris leaves and eat the inner tissue, eventually working their way down to the roots. In addition to seriously damaging the plants themselves, borers are often carriers of soft rot, one of the most serious diseases affecting irises.

Keeping iris beds free of debris will help prevent an infestation of borers. In early spring, spray young plants with dimethoate, malthion, or carbaryl.

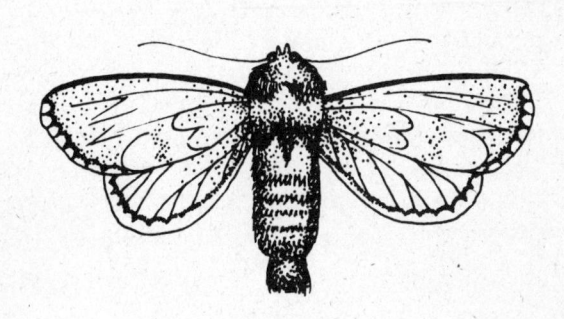

JAPANESE BEETLES

The Japanese beetle is about ½ inch long and easily recognized by its metallic bronze wing covers. Japanese beetles appear in hot weather and vigorously attack a wide range of plants, devouring leaves, buds and stems until only a skeleton remains.

If only a few beetles are visible, pick them off and drop them into a can of kerosene. If the infestation is severe, spray with malathion, carbaryl or methoxychlor. Milky spore disease is effective against the larvae.

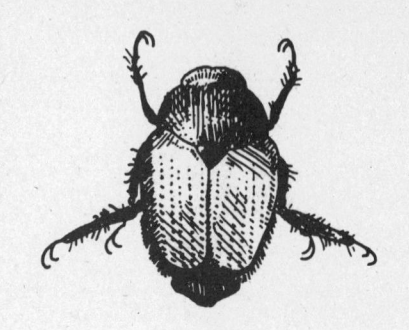

LEAF MINERS

Leaf miners are the larvae of various kinds of flies and beetles that lay their eggs between the two surfaces of leaves. The miners hatch out and devour the soft inner tissue of the leaves. Their presence is indicated by blotches, blisters or serpentine tunnels in the foliage.

To control miners, spray once a week for three weeks with malathion, diazinon, dimethoate or carbaryl. This kills the adults before they have a chance to lay eggs. No treatment is effective against the larvae themselves.

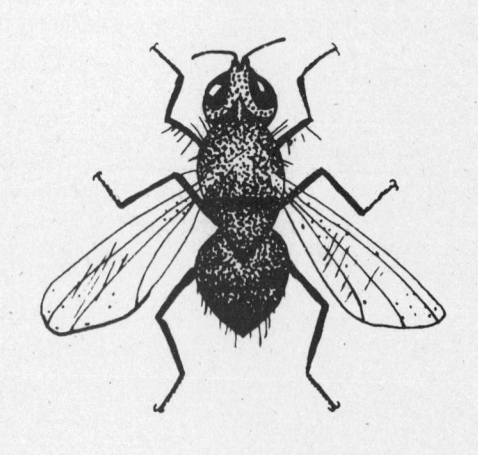

SPIDER MITES

Spider mite is about the size of a speck of paprika, but they are usually yellow or green instead of red. Even if you can't see the mites themselves, you will probably be able to see their white webs on the undersides of leaves. They seriously damage plants by sucking sap from the leaves. One of the smallest members of this family, the cyclamen mite, is one of the pests that attack delphiniums.

Spider mites can usually be dislodged with a hard jet of water. If this doesn't work, spray with a miticide, such as Kelthane, Tedion, or Omite.

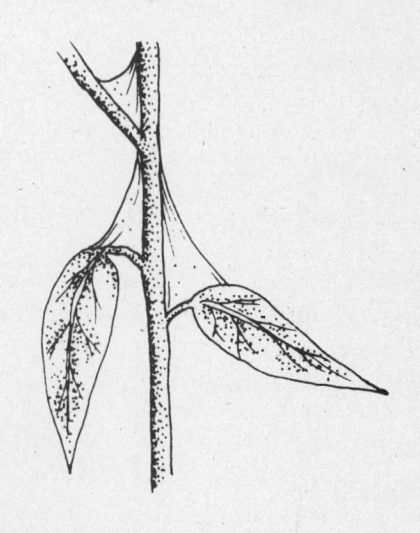

THRIPS

Thrips are minute insects with rasping mouth parts. They scrape away plant tissue and then suck out the sap. Their presence is indicated by deformed leaves and buds, and by distinctive brown or silvery streaks on leaves.

Spray with malathion or dimethoate. Repeat at two-week intervals if necessary.

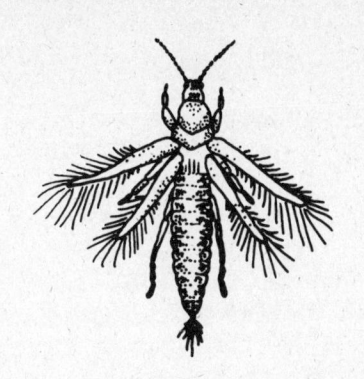

SNAILS AND SLUGS

Slugs are about twice as large as snails, and they have no shell. Both come out of hiding at night to feed on leaves and young shoots. They can do a surprising amount of damage.

To keep snails and slugs out of the garden, spread a strip of coarse sand or cinders around it. To trap and kill these pests, put out a saucer of beer or grape juice. They'll crawl into it and drown. If all else fails, put out metaldehyde bait or use zectran.

At Ease, Disease!

Just as many diseases attack perennials as any other plants and, though they rarely kill, they do damage and disfigure them. Remember that an ounce of prevention is worth a pound of fungicide. Below are some suggestions that should help you keep your perennials fit as a fiddle.

Don't plant in wet, shady places.

Don't crowd the plants together. Leave room for air circulation.

Water early in the day so leaves can dry before nightfall. Fungus diseases thrive on wet leaves.

Stake plants that need it, and keep all branches off the ground.

Remove and burn diseased leaves, stems and flowers. (Never put any of these in the compost heap.)

As soon as the plants become well established, apply a disease-preventive spray every 7 to 10 days and after heavy rains. Us a spray containing zineb or Bordeaux mixture; follow mixing instructions on the label.

To spread the spray evenly over leaf surfaces, add 1/3 teaspoon of synthetic detergent or mild soap to each gallon. Be sure to spray the undersurfaces of all leaves. Stop spraying when buds show color.

Prescription for Puny Perennials

Mildew, rust, bud rot, septoria leaf spot, and verticillium wilt may disfigure the leaves of chrysanthemums and other perennials. Each of these diseases is caused by a fungus that lives on the plant and all can be controlled with dusts or sprays. Mildew causes grayish-white powdery patches on the leaves. Later the leaves turn yellow and wither.

Control: As soon as the disease is noticed, dust the plant with finely ground sulfur. Repeat this treatment once a week until the buds show color.

Rust causes small, brown blisters on the undersurfaces of leaves. The area around each blister turns light green. The leaves eventually curl and die.

Control: Spray the plant with ferbam or dust with sulfur as soon as you notice the disease. Spray or dust once a week until the buds show color.

Bud rot causes the growing tip and bud to soften and turn brown. Affected buds do not open.

Control: Apply a spray containing zineb, Bordeaux mixture, or fermate every 7 days until just before the plant flowers.

Septoria leaf spot causes leaves to turn brown, reddish or yellow. Then black spots develop. Infection starts at the bottom of the plant and spreads upward.

Control: Spray plants with ferbam or Bordeaux mixture every seven to ten days; continue until buds show color.

Verticillium wilt is caused by a fungus that lives in the soil. Diseased plants usually wilt, turn brown, become stunted, and produce poor flowers. If the plants do not wilt, areas between the veins of the leaves turn yellow.

Control: Remove all infected plants and burn them.

A Fatal Stunt

Chrysanthemum stunt, aster yellows and leaf nematode infection prevent normal growth. There is no effective control for any of these. All severely stunted plants should be pulled up and burned immediately.

Chrysanthemum stunt is caused by a virus. Stunted, diseased plants will often bloom earlier than vigorous, healthy ones. Leaves may turn a reddish color or fade to light green.

This virus may be carried to healthy plants on a knife used to take cuttings, or even on your hands after you've pinched plants. You can prevent spreading by washing your hands thoroughly after touching any stunted plant. Also wash the cutting knife or better still, dip it in denatured alcohol.

Aster yellows is caused by a virus that is carried to chrysanthemums by leafhoppers. Indications of this disease are distorted flowers and many small, weak shoots. There is no known cure, but you should take preventive measures, especially if you plan to grow asters again in the future. Remove all weeds from the neighborhood of the aster bed. If you're really an aster afficionado, grow them in cloth-covered houses to keep out insects carrying the disease.

Leaf nematodes are microscopic, parasitic worms that feed on many garden plants. Chrysanthemums infected by nematodes have dark spots on the undersurfaces of the leaves. Also, they often have brown areas between the leaf veins. Plants become stunted and the buds fail to develop. The leaves wither and dry, but continue to hang on the stems after they're dead.

Nematodes are very persistent and can live 3 or more years in dead chrysanthemum leaves. They can also live for a long time in the soil. Cut and burn all infected plants — never put them in the compost heap. Do not plant healthy chrysanthemum plants in soil where diseased plants have grown. Wait at least 3 years or use a soil fumigant.

African marigolds have shown some ability to kill off nematodes in the soil due to sulfur containing substances exuded by their roots. As a test, marigolds were grown as the main crop in nematode-infected soil, and they were remarkably effective in reducing the infestation.

Propagation

Perennials are habit-forming. Once you start growing them, you want more and more. Unfortunately, your budget may put quite a crimp in your style. But don't despair. Perennials, aside from being beautiful, are very practical. Once you've established a good clump of your favorite perennial, you can easily propagate new plants from it — and they won't cost you a penny. Perennials can be propagated from root or stem cuttings or from divisions, depending on the variety you want to propagate and your preference.

Perennials may also be started from seeds, according to the method described earlier, but this often requires a great deal of patience. Many seed-started perennials take a long time to reach flowering size. Peonies, for example, may take as long as 7 years to bloom. However, some multiplying biennials must be started from seed. This group includes foxgloves, Canterbury bells, and wallflowers. Among the perennials which may be grown from seed are lupines, columbines, gas plants and delphiniums.

If Friends Give You the Slip

You can take stem cuttings from your own perennials or from your friends' — if your friends agree, of course. If you are planning to "borrow" some cuttings from a gardening friend, take a plastic bag along with you. After you've taken the cuttings, moisten them, place them in a plastic bag, and keep them as cool as possible until you can plant them.

The best time to take cuttings (or "slips," as Grandma Putt used to call them) is in spring or early summer. Take a sharp knife or pruning shears to the garden with you. Pick the plants you want to propagate and cut a 2- to 6-inch segment from the top of a mature stem. The cut should be made ¼ inch below a node, which is the joint at which a leaf joins the stem. If there is a bud or flower at the top of the cutting, pinch it off to encourage the cutting to devote all its energy to root production. Pinch off the lower leaves so that the bottom inch of the cutting will be bare. If the first cut you made is not clean, make a new one with a razor blade.

Don't try to root cuttings in the garden. It just won't work. You'll have to pamper your babies a little if you want them to grow big and strong. Flower pots, wood or plastic flats, peat pots or any other container at least 4 inches deep will make a good nursery for your cuttings. Whatever you use, just make sure it drains properly. Fill your container with a sterile rooting medium, such as perlite, vermiculite, shredded sphagnum moss, or sand. Wet the rooting medium thoroughly before inserting the cuttings. If you're using sand, tamp it after wetting, then wet it again.

Now that you have everything ready, dip the bottom end of each cutting into water, then into a powdered rooting stimulant. Shake off any excess. Poke as many inch-deep holes as you have cuttings in the rooting medium. Insert the cuttings, firm them in, and water thoroughly. Cover the container with a sheet of clear plastic and set it in a bright place. Keep the cuttings out of bright sun, though, or they'll cook.

Watch your cuttings closely. When new leaves appear, open the plastic so the young plants can get accustomed to fresh air. A few days later, carefully remove one of the cuttings from the rooting medium and examine the roots. If they're ½ inch long or longer, the plants are ready to move to the garden.

1

Choose a 2- to 6-inch segment at the top of a stem. Cut it ¼ inch below a node. Remove the leaves from the bottom inch of the cutting.

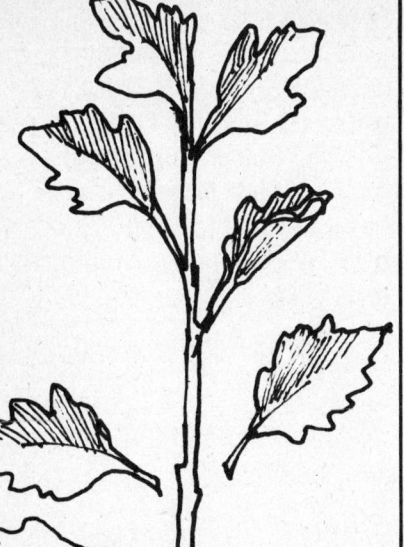

2

Dip the bottom end of each cutting into water, then into a powdered rooting stimulant. Shake off the excess.

3

Insert the cuttings into the sterile rooting medium with which you've filled your container. Firm the cuttings in and water thoroughly.

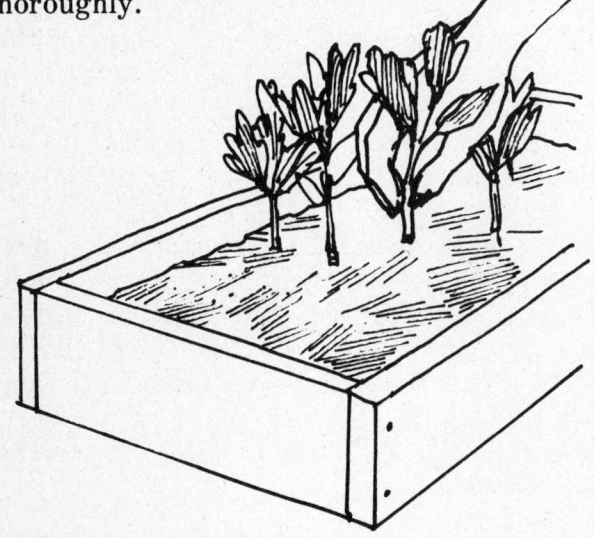

4

Cover the container with a sheet of clear plastic, or invert a plastic bag over it. Set in a bright place, but keep the cuttings out of direct sunlight.

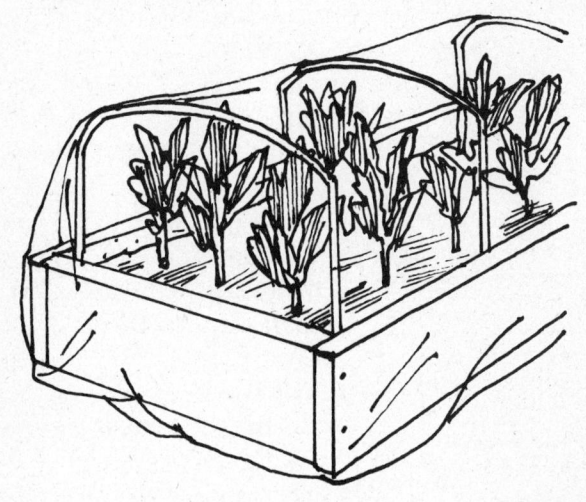

Getting to the Root of it

Some flowers, such as Japanese anemones, blanketflowers and butterfly weed, can be propagated from root cuttings. Basically, all you do is snip off 1- to 2-inch-long pieces of root when you lift a clump of perennials for dividing or transplanting. Once you've cut the pieces, fill a container with sand or garden soil. Lay the root pieces on their sides and cover them with ½ inch of soil or sand. Firm the surface and water carefully. Place the container in a cold frame over the winter. When the cuttings sprout in spring, move them to an outdoor kindergarten until they're large enough to take their permanent positions.

Slender Roots

1 When you dig up a clump of perennials in the fall, snip 1- to 2-inch-long pieces off the tips of the roots.

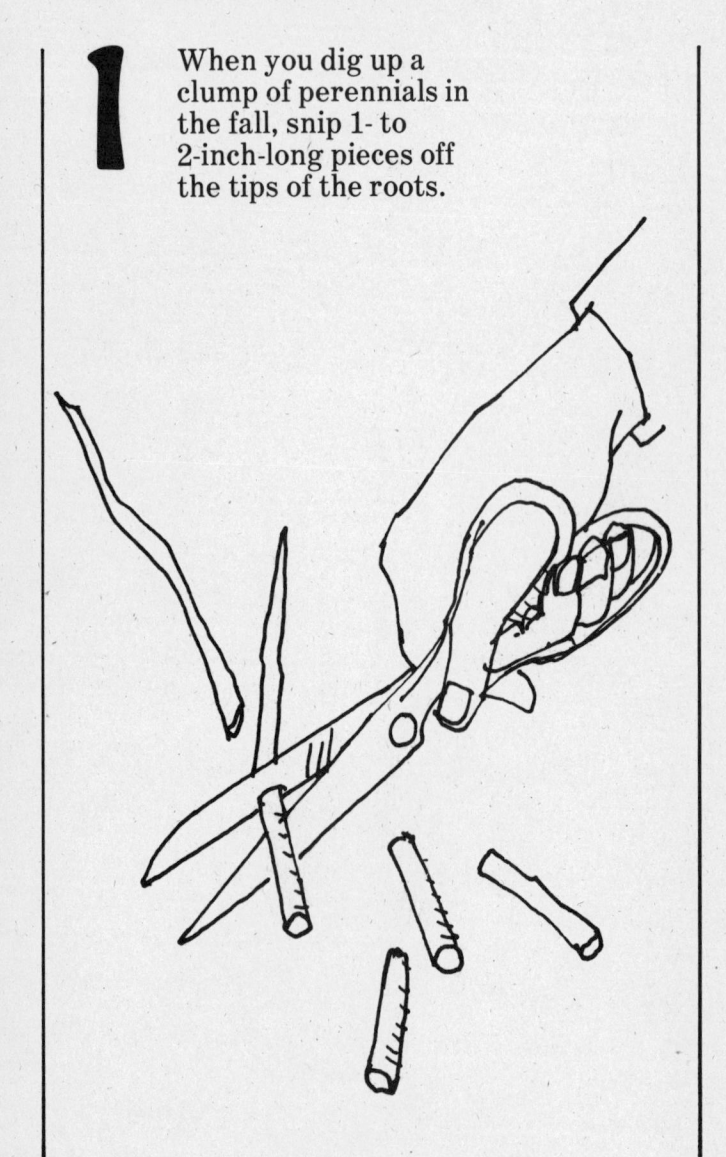

2 Lay the pieces in a container filled with sand or garden soil. Cover with ½ inch of soil or sand, firm them in, and water carefully. Leave the container in a cold frame until the cuttings sprout in spring.

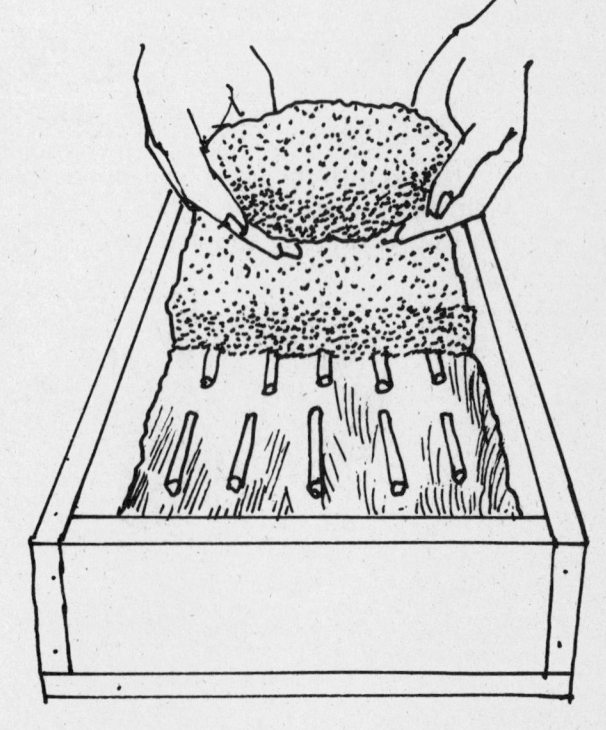

Some plants, such as bleeding hearts and Oriental poppies, require a different root-cutting technique. Cut 3- or 4-inch-long segments, and pot individually in 5- or 6-inch pots. The pieces should be in an upright position. To make sure you don't plant the pieces upside down, it's a good idea to mark the top of each piece as you cut it. Nick the top or make a straight cut across the top and a diagonal cut across the bottom. Plant the pieces so the top of each is ½ to 1 inch below the soil surface. Water carefully, then set the pots in a cold frame over the winter. In the spring, when sprouts appear, move the cuttings outdoors.

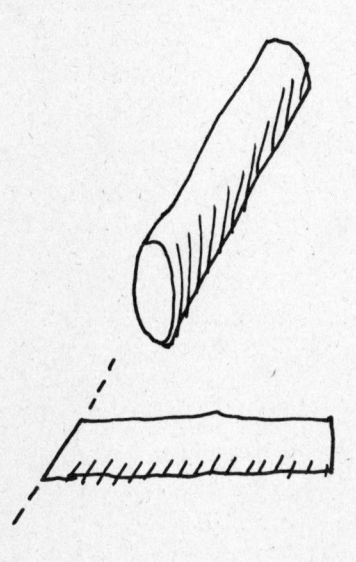

Thick Roots

1 Cut 3- or 4-inch-long segments of root, marking the top of each piece as you cut it. Nick the top or make a straight cut across the top and a diagonal cut across the bottom.

2 Plant each piece right-side-up in a 5- or 6-inch pot. The top of the cutting should be ½ to 1 inch below the soil surface. Leave the pots in a cold frame until sprouts appear in spring.

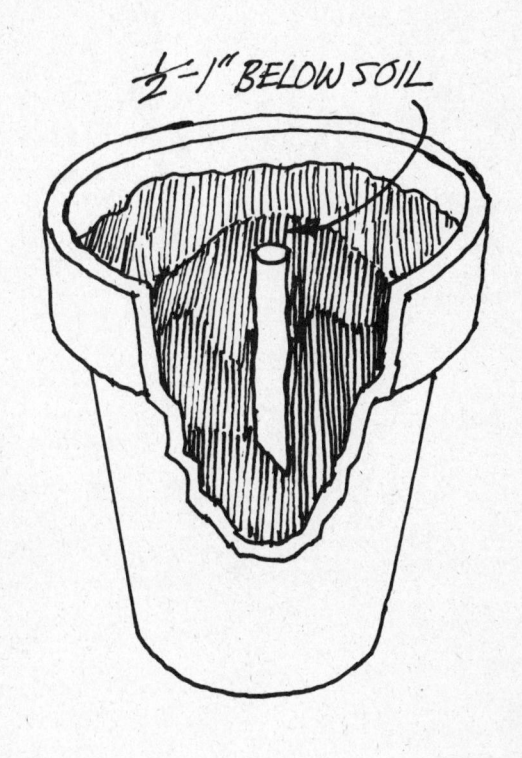

"Does this mean I have a split personality?"

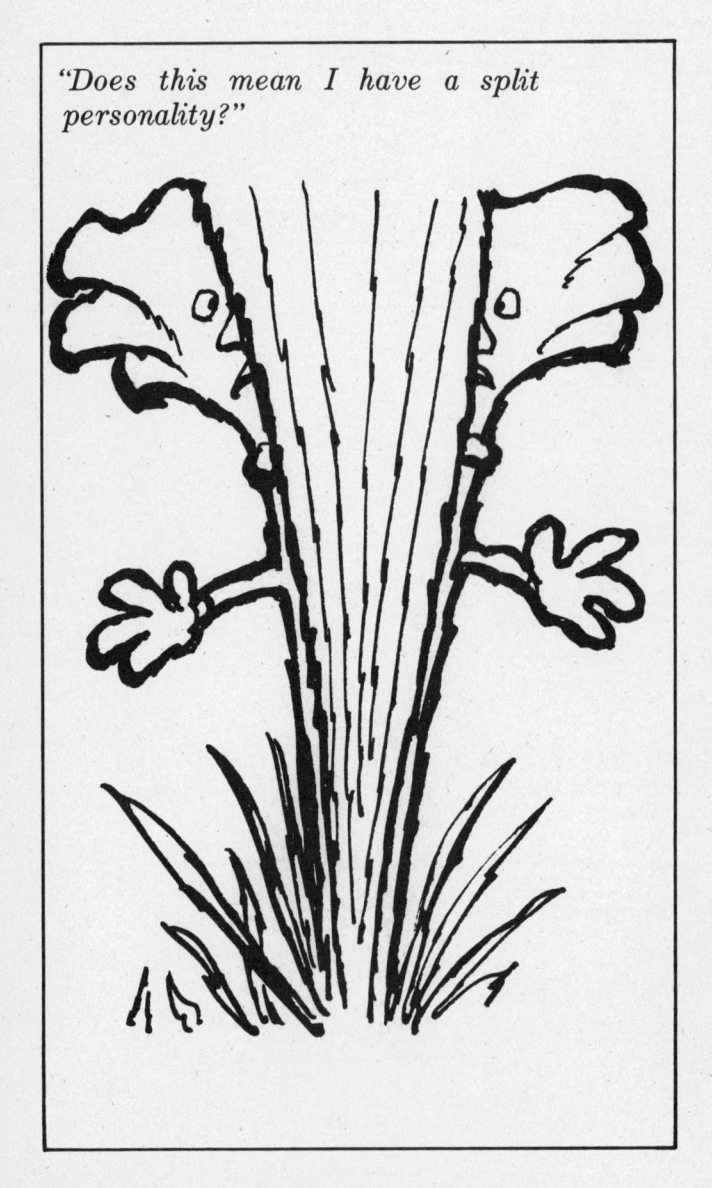

Divide to Conquer

You should plan to divide perennials every 3 years. If this is not done the center of the clump will grow poorly, and you will have few flowers. This is because the clump has begun to deplete the soil's fertility. In other words, the plant has begun to crowd itself.

To avoid having to remake all your perennial beds at once, plan to divide only a few at a time. This way, you will always have beds in bloom and new beds coming on.

When you are going to make divisions, select only the vigorous side shoots, the best outer parts of the clump. Discard the center, which is likely to be deficient in strength and grow-power. Divide the plant into clumps of 3 to 5 shoots each. Don't divide the clumps into too-small sections or you won't have much color the first year after replanting.

Divide perennials in the fall in southern areas and in the spring in northern areas.

Do not put all the divisions back into the same area that the original plant came from. They would soon become overcrowded, and the soil is probably depleted. Before planting any in the same place, spade a 3-inch layer of peat moss and a dusting of 0-20-20 fertilizer into the soil.

Give extra plants to friends or plant them in other locations about your property. Never throw any away. Maybe you could donate some to a school, hospital or nursing home in your community.

1

Shallow-rooted perennials, such as bee balm and fall aster, may be divided with a sparp spade. Cut sections containing 2 to 4 eyes or stems from the periphery of the plant. Discard the old center.

2

Some perennials, such as day lilies, have thick, tangled roots and are difficult to divide. Dig up the clump and insert 2 spading forks, back to back, into it. Carefully pry the roots apart.

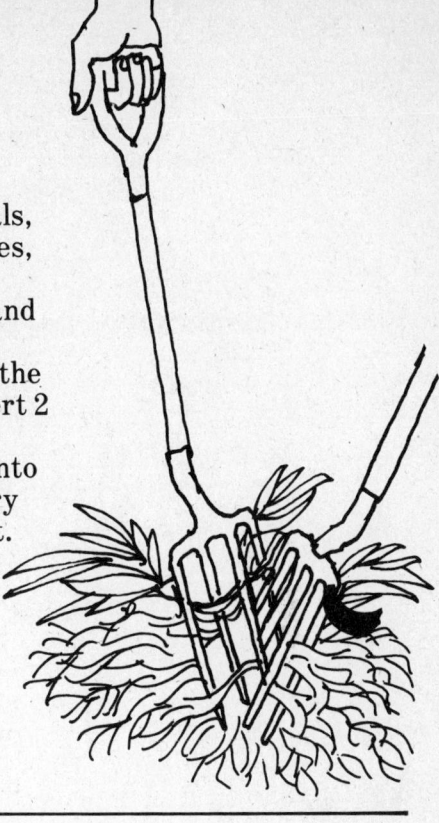

3

Primroses and several other small perennials are so shallow rooted that they can be divided by hand. Dig up a clump, shake off all loose soil, and pry the sections apart with your fingers.

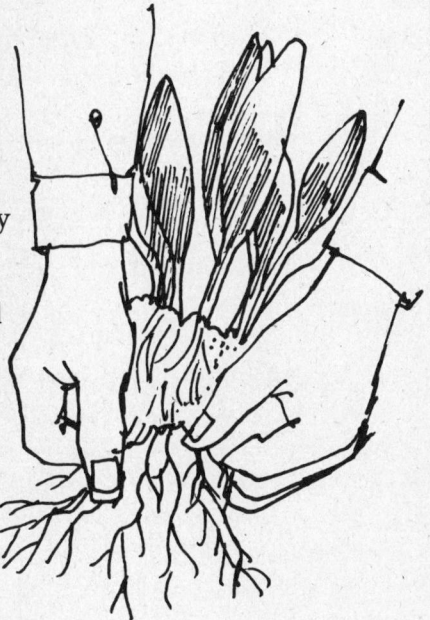

4

Do not put all the divisions back in the same area. Before planting any there, spade a 3-inch layer of peat moss and a dusting of 0-20-20 fertilizer into the soil.

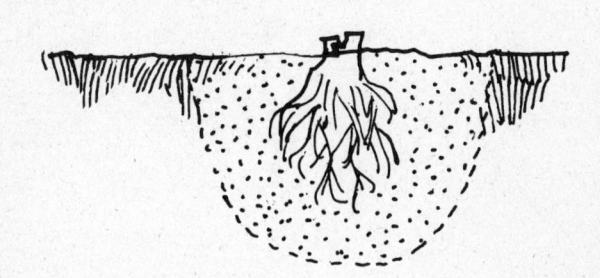

More Propagation Talk

Iris Demands a Place in the Sun

Few plants are as easy to grow as perennial iris. According to type, irises should be divided every 3 to 5 years. You will know by looking at them when they need dividing for the rhizomes will be heaving themselves out of the ground, literally growing on top of each other in their eagerness to get their share of the warm sun. Irises, growing as they do right on top of the ground, are easy to dig. Uproot the clump and separate it, retaining the strongest plants, usually those growing on the outside of the mass.

In most regions, the best time for doing this is from July to September, right after blooming time. But irises are so accomodating that separation may be done at almost any time. I have even separated clumps in early December and had many of them bloom the following year.

The newly separated rhizomes should be planted flat and only partially covered. They should never be deeply buried, for they must be sun-baked in order to produce masses of large blooms. The roots, which spread out from the rhizomes in all directions, should be covered with soil. Set new clumps in groups of three, with the tips of the rhizomes pointing to the outside of the clump. If the soil is very dry, it should be moistened. Irises are wonderful to place on a terrace or slope for erosion control.

You're Queen for a Day, Lily

The lovely day lilies are another vigorous-growing perennial, particularly useful for planting on slopes. They are exceedingly handsome, coming in a wide range of color and in dwarf and tall sizes.

Dig older clumps in either spring or fall and separate the pieces for replanting. I like to plant three of the tubers in a small clump, placing the clumps 18 to 24 inches apart, to achieve an attractive effect quickly.

One of the most interesting things about day lilies is another way in which the stock may be increased — by proliferation. On certain varieties, shortly after blossoming a joint about 4 to 5 inches below the flower head will start to put out small, slender leaves. Let this grow for a couple of weeks, then cut off the spent flower head just above this joint. Then cut the green stem about 6 inches below the joint and insert this in a cool moist, shaded spot. Push it down so that the base of the last leaf just touches the ground. Keep moist and the new plant will quickly put down a root system of its own, after which it may be transplanted to a permanent location. Keep a close watch each year, for these mischievous clowns are tricky. Some years, these plantlets seem to be more in evidence than in others. Sometimes plants which have never shown this tendency before will start doing it.

Day lilies are particularly useful for growing in hot, dry sections of the country. They will often stand up and bloom, day after day, when other flowers falter and give up.

Biennials

The difference between annuals, biennials and perennials is somewhat relative. Petunias, for instance, may be grown as annuals in the North, but often live over winter in the southern states and may be grown as perennials. A biennial, generally speaking, is a plant which may be expected to grow for two years, producing leaves the first year and flowers or fruit the second.

The hollyhock is one of the most important

Time runs out for Benny Biennial at the tender age of two.

Beautiful biennial hollyhocks are an impressive addition to any garden.

biennials (in some climates considered a perennial). This tall fellow will quite likely perpetuate himself by self-sown seeds.

The English daisy is — how confusing can you get? — a perennial which is usually treated like a biennial.

Canterbury bells are often grown from seeds and, with a little care, young seedlings may be safely transplanted. Foxgloves, forget-me-nots, and pansies are also considered biennials. Since pansies have long been spring favorites, I will give the directions for growing these lovely elves. Other biennials will prosper and delight you with the same general treatment.

I always think of pansies as the little old men of the garden. They remind me of Snow White's seven friendly dwarfs. They often seem to have angry little faces, grimacing in disapproval at the rest of the flowers. But these grumpy little men are just hiding their soft hearts and waiting for a friendly word. Tell them how nice they are, and just watch what brilliant colors they will display for you!

Pansies do best in rich, well-drained soil. So, before you plant the seeds, add manure, peat moss, or a 5-10-5 commercial fertilizer to the soil. If the soil is exceptionally heavy, dig in some sand. Spade the soil to a depth of 6 to 8 inches. Make sure it is fine and free of lumps, stones and other coarse materials.

If you plant seed in containers, select boxes 9 to 12 inches deep, and fill them with rich, sandy, loamy soil. Broadcast the seed or sow them in rows.

If you plant in open beds, sow seeds in rows about 4 to 6 inches apart. This will make it easier for you to identify the seedlings when they emerge, and it permits you to cultivate and weed more readily.

Whether you plant indoors or out, in frames or in open beds, water the seedbed first. Then, when the water has drained away, sow the seeds thinly. Cover the seeds with only an eighth of an inch of soil or coarse washed sand, and press down with a flat board. Water the bed again, but don't wash the seeds away. If possible, use the mister. Pansy seeds are very tiny.

← MOIST BURLAP

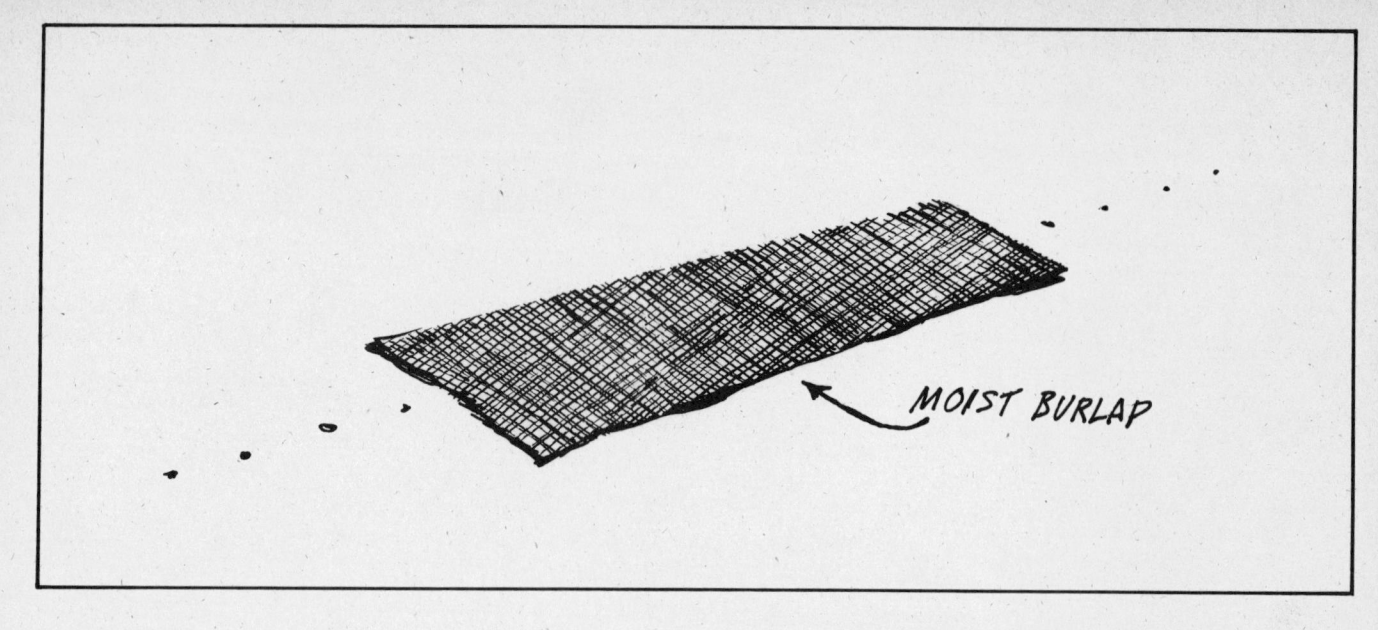

Plastic film, aluminum foil, or a piece of moist burlap placed on the seedbed will help keep moisture in. Remove this as soon as the seeds begin to sprout (in about 5 to 8 days). Shade the seedlings with a canopy for a few days until they develop their first true leaves. The canopy (an inexpensive, makeshift one will do) should be arranged a foot or two above the bed to let the air circulate.

Water lightly every morning. Seedlings should be neither too dry nor too wet. If the seed dries out after it begins to sprout, it will die; but if you keep it too moist, it may rot.

After the seedlings have emerged, thin them to an inch or more apart. Use care in removing the extras so that you will disturb the roots of those that remain as little as possible. Replant the seedlings you remove in another prepared bed.

The planting procedure for seedlings you buy is about the same as for seedlings you have grown yourself. When you bring them home, sprinkle them with water and let them stand a little while to restore lost moisture before planting. When planting, carefully separate and spread the roots. Press the soil firmly around the plants so that good contact will be made with the roots. But don't press the soil so tightly that it will harden and cake when dry.

Cover newly planted seeds with a sheet of plastic, aluminum foil, or moist burlap to keep them from drying out.

With most perennials and biennials, it is better for the home gardener to buy seed, seedlings, or plants than to attempt to grow plants from his own home-grown seeds. Where summers are hot and dry, it is best to start with new seedlings each year. In favorable climates you may propagate your own pansies by dividing old plants.

Guide to Perennials and Biennials

Acanthus

Acanthus is truly a perennial with great dignity. The graceful, ornamental leaves once served as designs for the capitals of the classic Greek Corinthian columns. So valued are the leaves, even by modern gardeners, that many remove the flower stalks as soon as they appear and grow the plants solely for the elegant foliage.

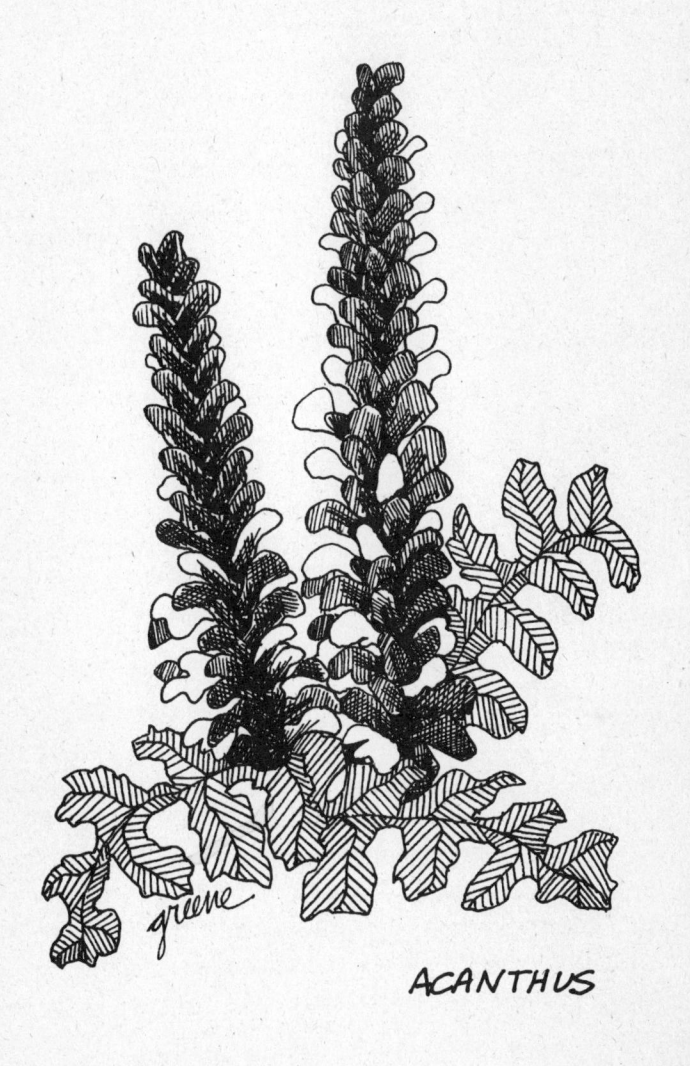

ACANTHUS

However, the spikes of white- or violet-tinted flowers, borne in the summer are also attractive, though less brilliant in color than many other perennials.

There are several species of acanthus, varying in height from 2 to 4 feet. It is useful for a shrub border, a wild garden or for naturalizing on the edge of a woodland.

Plants will flourish in a sunny or partially shaded place in well-drained, ordinary soil. Seed grow slowly, so separate rooted pieces for replanting.

Adonis (Amur Adonis)

The Greeks had a legend for this flower, too. It was believed that the plant sprang up from the blood Adonis shed when he was wounded by a wild animal. You would expect adonis to be red and it is. But there are also shades of white, pink, orange, yellow and copper.

It is one of the first flowers to appear in the spring. Blossoms often appear when the stems are only 3 to 4 inches tall, and they continue to grow and flower up to 15 to 18 inches in height.

Adonis likes a sandy soil enriched with ample leaf mold or compost. It will tolerate sun or light shade and is fine for a sunny border or for naturalizing in a woodland. Propagate by lifting plants in October, separating them into several pieces, and replanting.

Artemesia

Artemesias are enchanting, feathery-foliage plants whose silvery, gray-green leaves mix well in the perennial border and add charming contrast to cut flowers.

Artemesia Silver King averages 3 feet tall, and the white flowers are rather humble letting the foliage take all the bows. Silver Mound has silver leaves and slender stems. It will form a dense mound about a foot tall and spread out an equal distance. It makes an excellent edging for a perennial border.

Artemesias have another good quality — many are refreshingly aromatic. The delicate foliage, surprisingly long-lasting, is also frequently used in dried bouquets.

Artemesias are easily grown, preferring a moist but well-drained soil of average fertility. They may be propagated by root divisions. They are often such vigorous growers that dividing the clumps each fall and spring may be advisable.

Aster

In Greek aster means "star" — and that's just what the blossoms look like. These plants, sometimes called Michaelmas daisies, are very easy to grow. They will thrive in practically any good garden soil, spreading quickly into large clumps. Leave them undisturbed in the same spot for 2 or 3 years, and you will be rewarded with a real thicket. They will deplete the soil of nutrients and the flowers will grow increasingly smaller. Take the clumps up and divide them, using the best parts of the outer portions for replanting elsewhere. To have large clumps look their best, stake them in early summer.

Butterfly Weed (Asclepias tuberosa)

This very handsome member of the milkweed family is one of the most gorgeous bits of color in the perennial border. The large, fragrant clusters of brilliant orange flowers are carried high on the 2- to 3-foot-tall stems. As might be expected from the name, butterfly weed is frequently surrounded when in full bloom by such hordes of butterflies that it is sometimes called the "Butterflies' Mecca".

This plant is probably called a weed because it grows wild in many sections of this country and in southern Canada.

Plant seeds in the spring, choosing a sunny spot. The area should be well-drained and, if possible, sandy. Because of its long taproot, the butterfly weed can withstand long periods of drought. Also because of the long taproot, clumps do not transplant successfully. Once established, they should remain permanently undisturbed.

Bleeding Heart (Dicentra)

Bleeding heart is one of the plants your grandmother grew and loved, but they are just as beautiful now as in the gardens of long ago. The rosy, deep-red, sometimes "candy pink" hearts arch out above the light green foliage in May.

Plant bleeding hearts in the border where they will be lightly shaded. The plants will grow more vigorously and bear more and larger blossoms if the soil is enriched with organic matter.

Bleeding heart, while usually planted outdoors, is also a good subject for forcing in the spring. Plants may be potted in autumn and kept in a cool greenhouse for spring flowering.

For best results with this plant, leave it alone once it has become established. Not a rampant grower, it may go for many years without division.

BLEEDING HEART

Blanketflower (Gaillardia)

Blanketflower, sometimes called "firewheel," is truly brilliant. Somewhat resembling a large daisy, it has a purple disk in the center and red, yellow-tipped petals. Most gaillardias are native to the central and western United States, but are widely grown by gardeners in many areas. According to the section, gailliardia may be an annual, biennial or a perennial. Some types grow 2 to 3 feet tall.

Gaillardias will grow from cuttings or seeds, depending on the type. This gay flower will last from early summer till frost if no seed heads are allowed to form. It will even continue to bloom after a light frost in the autumn.

Leaves on gaillardias are somewhat scanty, and for this reason it should always be planted among foliage plants. They like the sun and will do well in any good garden soil.

Babies' Breath (Gypsophila)

The tiny blossoms of babies' breath, profusely borne on gracefully branched, feathery stalks, are truly exquisite. Not particularly showy alone in the garden, it is enchanting when planted among other flowers, and it is lovely in bouquets. Grown in borders, it has a softening, mistlike effect.

The continually dividing branches will grow from 1 to 3 feet tall. The leaves are smooth, sharp-pointed and light green.

The perennial species does best in full sun, preferring well-drained neutral soil, which may even lean a bit to alkaline. For best results, you should add lime if your soil is acid.

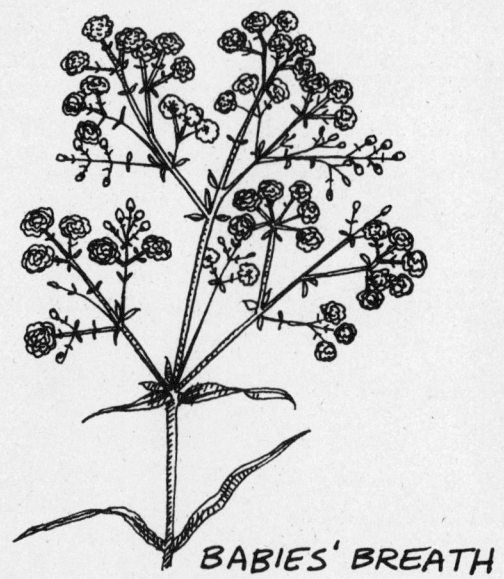

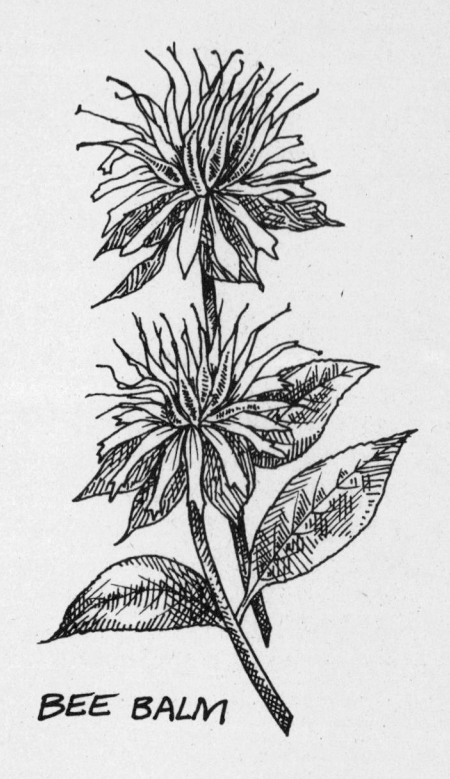

Bee Balm (Monarda alpestris)

Few flowers surpass the bee balm in brilliant color. A rather coarse plant when viewed close-up, it is very attractive when grown in large masses and is fine for naturalizing in open meadows.

Blooming occurs during the summer months. For the most dramatic effect, plant the scarlet, very fragrant bee balm against a dark background. The large heads are borne on stalks 2 to 4 feet high.

There are also white, rose-colored, and purple varieties.

Bee balm will grow in full sun or light shade. Not particular as to soil, they will appreciate the addition of organic material.

Always remove faded flowers before they can produce seeds to prolong the blooming period. Start new plants from clump divisions. Divide every 3 to 4 years to prevent crowding and to encourage larger blossoms.

Balloon flower (Platycodon)

Many flowers are named for some special characteristic; this blue boy has buds that swell up into tiny balloons just before he decides to unfold the starry petals. There is also a white species.

Growing only 12 to 18 inches tall, balloon flowers are charming for borders or rock gardens. They should be set 1 to 2 feet apart to allow for their rather spreading growth.

The pretty blue or white flowers are borne in July and August. Balloon flowers will flourish in sunny or lightly shaded locations. Once established, they dislike being disturbed. A well-mannered, polite plant, the clumps do not ramble but remain where you tell them to stay.

Sow seeds in a flat or sifted, sandy soil in a slightly heated greenhouse or coldframe in the spring. As soon as seedlings are well rooted they may be planted outdoors where they are to grow.

BALLOON FLOWER

Bellflowers

It has been said that the most difficult color for Nature to produce is blue. If that is true bellflowers are one of Mother Nature's best efforts. Carpathian bellflowers, for example, are a lovely blue and they are among the easiest flowers to grow. It is also very permanent and low-growing in habit, making neat, dainty clumps of foliage from 4 to 6 inches high.

Most bellflowers are hardy perennials or biennials that thrive in rich, well-drained, sunny garden soil. Start them from seed in early spring. Transplant outdoors about the middle of May and allow about 9 inches of space between the plants.

The tubular, bell-shaped flowers of Canterbury bells come in the traditional blue, but also in purple, pink and white. The loose-spreading spikes will brighten your garden to July. The plants are considered biennials, flowering the second year from open-sown seed.

Creeping bellflower is the riotous, rampantly growing member of the family often found rambling over the tumbledown fences of old, abandoned farmhouses. The flowers, a lovely violet-blue, are in evidence from July to September. The plant averages 2 to 4 feet tall and makes a lovely blue background. Set this boy to work in any unsightly area that needs to be covered quickly — he will dive right into the job with joyful abandon.

Centaureas

All members of the Centaurea family are good natured and accomodating, presenting few problems of culture if given a sunny location and good soil. They often do amazingly well even in poor soil and partial shade.

The amiable little cornflower is almost too friendly. Once established in your garden, it will self-sow and appear year after year. He means well and only wants to please you. If you get along well together, just thin the plants and enjoy his presence.

Sweet sultans grow about 2 feet tall and have flower heads like giant cornflowers. They do not like to be moved, so plant them where they are to grow permanently.

Chrysanthemums (including Shasta and Painted Daisies)

The Chrysanthemum family is large and popular. It includes shasta and painted daisies. The perennial chrysanthemums, which take first honors as autumn-flowering plants, have been cultivated so long that their origin has been forgotten. However, they are believed to be natives of China and southern Japan, and we are reasonably sure that they were cultivated in China some 500 years before the birth of Christ.

Modern chrysanthemums are classified according to the form of their bloom and also by their growth habits. There are many variations which include singles, semi-doubles, pompons, spoons, quills, spiders and threads, to name but a few. The cascades are very useful for growing in pots or baskets, literally forming a fountain of flowers.

CHRYSANTHEMUMS

Garden-grown chrysanthemums of the larger types should always be staked and tied or the immense blooms of the really big ones will fall over and look unsightly.

Christmas Rose (Helleborus niger)

The lovely, almost legendary Christmas rose is a real garden treasure. The snow-white flowers appear in late autumn or even early winter if the weather is mild. To insure good bloom development when cold weather threatens, cover the plants with a jar or a small cold frame.

The Christmas rose likes a partially shaded position and soil enriched by the addition of leafmold or compost. Try to place it in a permanent position from the very beginning, for the beautiful plants may be spoiled by shifting them too frequently.

The best time for planting is early spring. Set the plants 12 inches apart and plan for them to stay there for 6 to 7 years. If moving must be done, the best time is during September when they are making new roots.

Chinese Peonies (Paeonia)

The peony has much to recommend it — a healthy, hardy nature, vigorous growth, and, above all, beautiful, fragrant flowers. And the culture of these lovelies has advanced tremendously in recent years. Its honorable ancestors, the white albiflora and the red officinalis, would scarcely recognize it as their offspring today. Both of these species, Chinese in origin, were introduced into England as long ago as 1548.

At maturity, Chinese peonies will often reach 4 feet in height. These truly dignified mandarins of the garden produce handsome flower heads that may be as much as 10 inches across. Colors range from snowy white through pale yellow, to vibrant shades of pink or deep red. They may be double or single. The singles, with one row of five or more petals, are especially exquisite because of the central mass of pollen-bearing, golden stamens.

Soil for peonies should have large amounts of well-decomposed organic matter incorporated into it. Purchase named root divisions for best results.

CHINESE PEONIES

COLUMBINE

Columbine (Aquilegia)

Columbines are among the loveliest of garden flowers. Dancing on airy stems, nodding and smiling or making a dignified curtsy, they look like a welcoming committee as they hold court in the bed or border.

The many-colored flowers are always a welcome sight in spring and early summer. The deeply lobed green to blue-green foliage is also attractive, and the clump has a nice rounded manner of growth. Blossoms of the larger species may be as large as 4 inches across; the small ones 1½ inches. They provide a feast of nectar for hummingbirds.

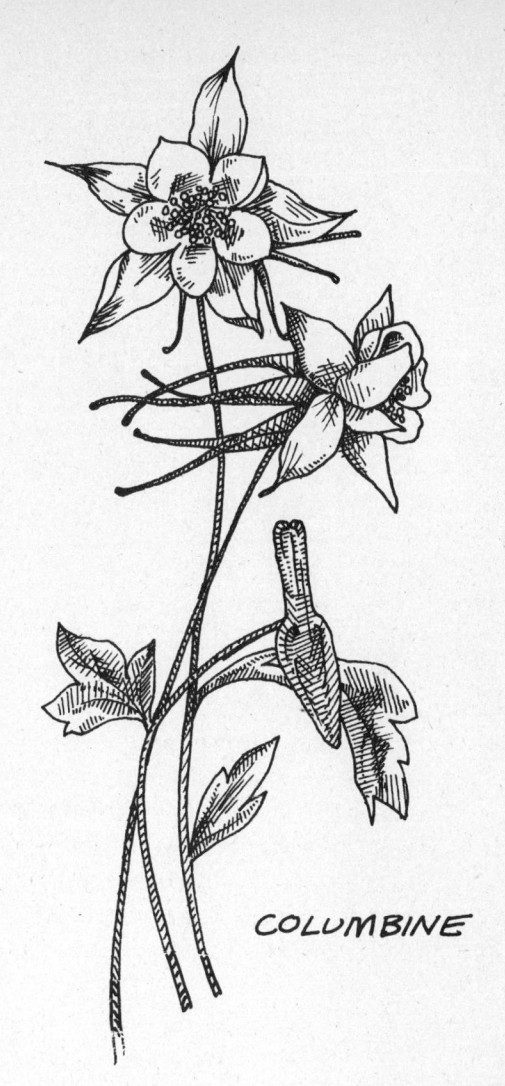

Purchase seeds from a reliable seedsman. If they are sown in summer, they will provide flowering plants the following spring. They prefer moist but well-drained soil in very light shade.

Crown Vetch (Coronilla)

These plants belong to the pea family, and may be either annual or perennial. They have deeply cut leaves, purple or yellow pea-shaped blossoms, and may grow from 1 to 9 feet in height. The low-growing types are nice for borders.

They like a sunny, well-drained location in light, sandy soil. They may be propagated by sowing seeds in pots of sandy soil in early spring and planting outdoors in late spring. Cuttings may also be made in June from older plants and inserted in the cold frame. Many types are suitable for planting in rock gardens.

Coral Bells (Heuchera sanguinea)

This is dainty little flower with bright, coral-red spikes which appear in July and continue to bloom on and off for the rest of the season.

Day Lily

Once upon a time, day lilies were either yellow or a rather harsh shade of orange, but no more. They come in a wide range of colors, some of the loveliest being the melon shades, often with shadowy violet tints. The season of bloom has also been extended from early spring until frost. Blossom size, in some particularly spectacular species, has been enlarged to 8 inches across.

Day lilies like their heads in the sun, but their roots appreciate moisture and rich soil. Each flower only lasts one day, but new ones open progressively, so the season of bloom is very long. The roots are bundles of fleshy tubers and are easily divided.

DELPHINIUM

DAY LILY

Delphinium

Delphinium, possibly the stateliest of all blue-flowered perennials, rightly deserves to be called the master of ceremonies. His impressiveness, distinction and importance are unquestioned as he towers over the rest of the plants, keeping a close watch on all that goes on.

Though there are other colors, the varieties which range in color from soft blue to deep blue are still the favorites, with whites, purples and lavenders drawing increasing attention.

Most delphiniums grow from 2 to 4 feet in height, but one, the candle delphinium, has stalks which may reach 6 feet. Allow delphiniums plenty of room, particularly the very tall ones whose massive spikes are composed of 2- to 3-inch flowers.

The principal flowering season is in June and early July, but they will flower again in the fall if the flowers are cut after the first blooming season. Let as much foliage as possible remain. When new shoots are well started, the old stalks may be cut down.

Young plants may be seriously damaged in spring by slugs. Ashes sifted around and among the shoots will help to prevent damage. If you prefer, use a mixture of equal parts of copper sulphate and hydrated lime. Scatter this on the soil but do not let it touch the plants.

ENGLISH DAISY

English Daisy (Bellis perennis)

These delightful dwarfs have large double or semi-double flowers in many shades of red and pink, as well as white.

These daisies will flourish in ordinary garden loam, provided it will retain moisture sufficient to their modest needs. Lift the plants in early summer as soon as the flowers have faded, separate the clumps into pieces, and replant 3 inches apart where they will not be exposed to full sunshine.

Evergreen Candytuft (Iberis sempervirens)

Who wouldn't love a little perennial with such a charming name as "candytuft"? And it is everything its name implies, for its sugar white blossoms are never melted by sunshine. Hardy, of easy culture, succeeding in any soil, in sun or partial shade—who could ask for more?

The flowers occur in big clusters, the outer ones being a bit larger than the inner ones. The narrow, lustrous, dark green leaves are truly evergreen, giving the border a neat look even when the blossoms are no longer in evidence.

The plants grow 6 to 9 inches tall and may spread 2 feet across. Some of the newer types will blossom in fall as well as spring.

Forget-Me-Not (Myosotis)

This little blue elf with bright yellow eyes should be welcomed into every garden. Understand his simple needs and you will never be without him. First of all, remember that he has no liking for hot weather and will get most of his blossoming out of the way by May. If his feet are in good, moist, organically enriched soil, he may last through the month of June. A lot depends on just how comfortable you make him.

He is most at home in cool and shady places, but an extremely wet place is not necessary. Make the seedbed very fine, and do not sow the seeds more than half an inch deep. Old plants may be divided or cuttings taken from them in the fall.

Four O'Clock (Mirabilis jalopa)

This funny fellow has a real sense of humor. He opens in late afternoon—if not exactly at four o'clock. Nobody knows why, but he is very determined about this — a real individualist.

The flowers may be white, pink, red, yellow or violet. This is a marvelous plant for planting where you can enjoy it in the evening, for the fragrant flowers will perfume the air all night long.

The plants, which may grow as tall as 3 feet, will remain in continuous blossom over a long period of time. They will survive over winter in mild climates. Farther north, plants may be dug in the fall and stored in a frost-proof place. Spring-planted seeds will usually blossom by mid-summer, so it may also be treated as an annual. Four o'clocks prefer full sun and a well-drained location.

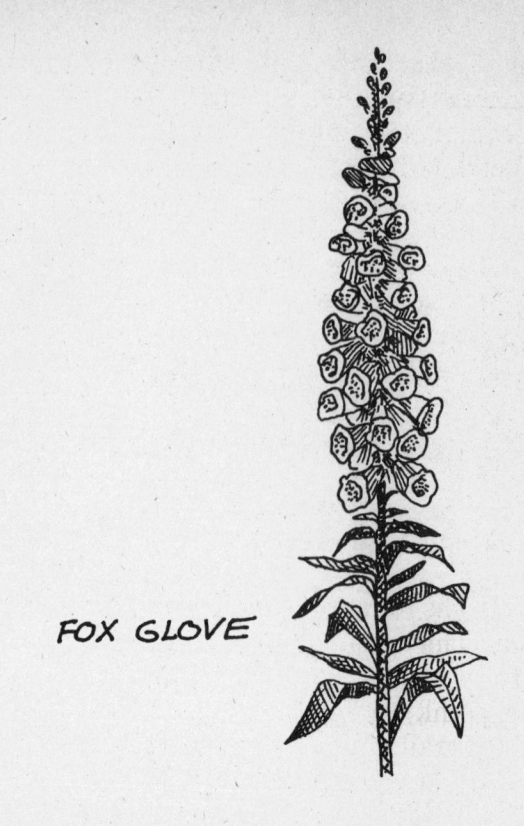

FOX GLOVE

FOUR O'CLOCK

Foxglove (Digitalis)

Vying for honors with the blue delphiniums, the foxgloves provide spires in another range of colors—white, yellow, pink, rose, purple and rusty red. Growing from 4 to 6 feet tall, they are almost as tall as delphiniums. But they are by no means second class citizens. The gloxinia-flowered strain is particularly remarkable.

Foxgloves, in most zones, are best treated as biennials, or short-lived perennials. In mild climates they may be grown in full sun or partial shade, but in hot, dry areas some shade will be necessary. They prefer moist, but well-drained soil.

Perennial foxgloves are most frequently grown from seeds, but new plants may be started by dividing and resetting older clumps.

Gazania

Gazanias are true "flower children," for they love to dance and play in the sun. Each 5-inch flower usually has 4 or 5 distinct, sharply-defined colors. The striking blossoms are framed by cool, gray-green foliage which forms a compact, 6-inch plant. If you live in a hot, dry climate, this is the flower for you. They will retain their crisp freshness all through the most arid summer.

Perhaps the most unusual of all is Fire Emerald, rivaling the rainbow in colors. Most of these blossoms have an emerald green center ring which adds to the striking display.

Gazanias love full sun and well-drained ground. They grow easily from seeds and may blossom all year in mild climates. Older clumps may be divided every 3 or 4 years.

Gerbera Daisy

Gerberas are a gift to us from South Africa. They are generous in flowering and produce blossoms in cream, yellow, orange-pink, crimson, purple and violet, all on long stalks fine for cutting. The leaves, which form a rosette close to the soil, are deeply lobed, lance-shaped and about 12 inches long.

Gerberas, as their origin would indicate, are best grown outdoors in the mild climate of the South, but may be enjoyed elsewhere if grown in greenhouses. They like full sun but prefer a moist, well-drained soil.

They may be propagated by division of older clumps in spring when they become overcrowded, by cuttings, or by seeds. Plant 12 to 15 inches apart.

Gloriosa Daisy (Rudbeckia)

These splendid, hard-working flowers are just great for a summer garden. They vary somewhat in height, some growing as tall as 5 feet, others only 2. Think where they will fit best in your landscape plan before making a selection. You may even want to put them in your cutting garden, for their 12- to 15-inch stems make them ideal for arrangements.

The perennial rudbeckias become established quickly, provide a display of color the first year, and bloom dependably thereafter.

They will thrive in well-drained, ordinary garden soil, but if you would really please, place them in full sun. The roots may be planted in fall or early spring—the sooner the better.

Hollyhock (Althaea rosea)

That humble favorite, the hollyhock, is possibly one of the oldest flowers in our garden. It was originally a native of China, but it has been grown so long and has become so common in the United States that most of us have forgotten its origin.

The original hollyhock was a single flower, but after hundreds of years of cultivation it now has many colors and variations of blossom, some being fully double. The flowers, growing all along the stem, are round and open wide. They range from white through yellow, salmon, red, and purple. Most hollyhocks are biennials, growing one year and blooming the next. They thrive in rich, well-drained soil and full sun. They will bloom longer if faded flowers are promptly removed.

Heart-Leaved Bergenia (Bergenia)

Bergenias are handsome plants useful in the perennial border. Their greatest appeal lies in their handsome, heart-shaped leaves and their clusters of dainty blossoms. These are borne in spring on dancing stems just above the foliage. The leaves are 8 to 10 inches across with saw-toothed edges and are of a rich, deep green.

Bergenias will flourish in any good garden soil in full sun or light shade. If grown in a hot, dry area, shade is preferable. They do best in a soil enriched with humus, but are tolerant of a wide range of soil conditions. They are excellent for naturalizing beside a brook or pool, for they do not mind having their feet wet.

New plants can be started by division, older clumps usually being divided every 3 or 4 years.

Hardy Ageratum (Eupatorium coelestirum)

If you are looking for a plant with a multitude of uses, ageratum is your boy. Sometimes called floss flower or mist flower, this persistent bloomer is equally at home in sun or shade. Not terribly particular as to soil, the soft blue, fluffy blossoms will carpet fall flower beds, manfully edge a border, grace a rock garden, or present a pretty show in window or porch boxes. And by potting a few plants in the fall, you can enjoy the bright blooms in winter.

Always in a hurry to please, he will start to bloom a scant 3 months after the seed is sown. Remove the faded blooms and the season of blossoms will be greatly lengthened.

Also in a hurry to spread, he will move rapidly along under the ground and spring up everywhere if soil conditions are favorable. You may need to scold him a little occasionally and pull up plants which ramble over into someone else's territory.

Iris

So varied and beautiful are irises in all their forms and colors that many people like to make collections of them. With some thought given to the different periods of blooming, the season may be extended all through spring and early summer. There are even fall blooming varieties. The tall bearded irises bloom toward the end of May and are the most important group for garden use. The earliest to bloom are the dwarf bearded irises. A little while after these come the purple flag irises often seen in old gardens. Listed among the intermediate irises are also those which sometimes surprise us by blooming in September and October.

And don't overlook the beardless irises. Among these are the truly magnificent Japanese Irises.

And then there are the bulbous irises which have Spanish, English and Dutch representatives. There is also a miscellaneous group which includes the strange Oncocylus.

Italian Bugloss (Anchusa azurea)

If you love the delicate blue blossoms of forget-me-nots, you will also love anchusa, which performs much the same function for the sunny summer border. If you will start the perennial type early, it will bloom the first year, providing a showy fountain of brilliant blue color.

The bright blossoms of anchusa are very attractive to bees, which seem to be constantly hovering over a planting.

Anchusas will flourish in any well-drained garden soil. They prefer a sunny spot. Somewhat unattractive after blooming, you may cut them off and get a smaller display of blossom in the fall.

Lavender (Lavendula)

A famous feature of old English gardens were the lavender walks, and the fragrant, beloved blossoms are still sold in London streets. But here in America, lavender is not hardy very far north, though it may be grown for a sweet summer border.

Though we have come to think of lavender as belonging to England, it is actually a native of the Mediterranean region where it grows on dry, hilly, open wasteland. To be successful with it, take care to plant it in similar conditions in your own garden insofar as possible. Be particularly careful to avoid excessive moisture, and occasionally lime the soil. Lavender is an excellent choice for rock gardens.

The delicate silvery gray leaves produce the same delightful scent as the flowers when they are rubbed. Foliage as well as flowers have long been dried to make sweet-smelling potpourris and sachets for linen closets.

Lavender may be grown from either seeds or stem cuttings.

Lily Turfs (Liriope muscari)

Liriope muscari, sometimes called big blue lily turf, grows 12 to 18 inches tall, forming a clump of grass-like leaves which may attain a length of 2 feet. It is excellent for borders in the warmer sections of the country, where it will remain evergreen all winter.

While most liriope is blue, there is also a white variety. Varigata has blue flower spikes, but the foliage is edged with pale yellow or white.

Creeping lily turf spreads by means of underground runners. Because they will tolerate a wide range of growing conditions, they are very useful as ground cover plants. Space them about 12 inches apart and propagate by dividing and resetting older clumps in the spring.

Lupine (Lupinus)

Lupines rank with the top perennials in garden value. Their stately, spectacular spires, which are magnificent when grouped among other flowers, will mark you as a gardener who understands his landscaping.

The lupines are true majordomos, standing straight and tall. They expect many of the other flowers to look up to them and appreciate their worth. They, in turn, guard the territory with diligence, permitting no trespassers.

Probably the most gorgeous garden treasures of all are Russell's Hybrids, whose exciting colors are perfectly set off by their deep-green, cut-leaved foliage.

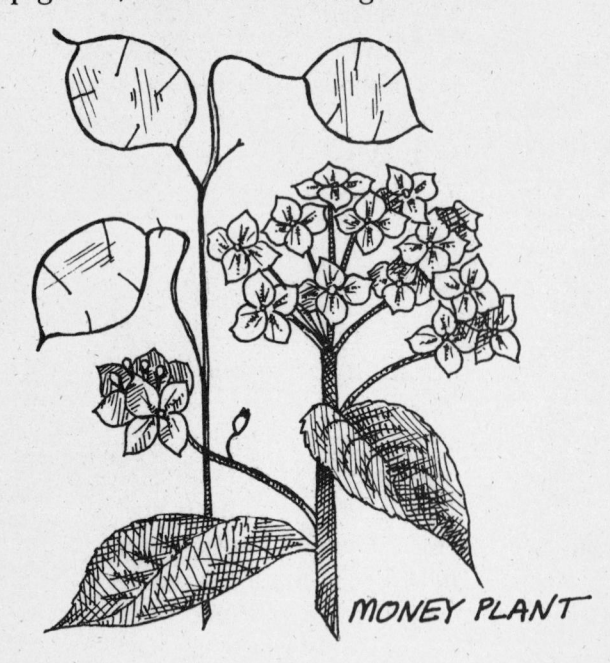

Money Plant (Lunaria)

Lunaria, called by the various names of honesty, dollar plant, and St. Peter's penny, is the keeper of the treasury. He grows his own money in the form of flat paperlike seed pods, which are frequently used in combination with other dried material in winter arrangements. These rounded, translucent pods follow the fragrant clusters of purple, pink or white blossoms which grace the plant in late spring and early summer.

Space plants 12 to 15 inches apart in full sun or light shade. Well-drained soil is preferred. Honesty makes an honest effort to propagate itself. It sows its own seeds year after year, and so keeps the treasury full and operating.

Oriental Poppy (Papaver orientale)

The Oriental poppy, I think, more nearly resembles a Spanish dancer with flashing, full skirts. They are constantly urged by the wind to nod and sway and curtsy gracefully on their long stems. The showy buds issue from the ground on strong stems which may attain a height of 3 feet. They are true show stoppers and occupy the center of the stage while they are in bloom.

It is not difficult to raise the plants from seed, though there may be some variability in color and size. Most seedlings are likely to have orange-red flowers. Root cuttings may also be taken in spring. Oriental poppies do not like to be disturbed, so plant them where they are to remain indefinitely.

Pampas Grass (Cortaderia selloana)

This vaquero, native to Argentina, is widely grown throughout the Southwest and will grow much farther north if placed in a protected area. I am a great admirer of pampas grass, and, while many recommend it for the back of the shrub border, I prefer to use it as a specimen plant. The impressive silvery-white to pink plumes stand tall and proud, riding high above the tough, sawtoothed leaves. If you are determined to make your South American cowboy pay his way, let him do what he does best — ride the line as a fast-growing windbreak.

Hard-working, he will do well in any soil, wet or dry. All he asks is that his location be sunny. Pampas grass may be increased by dividing the clumps or by sowing the seeds in a greenhouse in early spring.

The flower plumes, which appear in late summer and early fall, are frequently cut and used for winter decorations. The best flowers grow on female plants. Your nurseryman will know which is which.

SWEET WILLIAMS

Pink and Sweet Williams (Dianthus)

Just about every plant that is grown in our gardens year after year has some outstanding feature by which it maintains its popularity. The many members of the dianthus family not only produce lovely blossoms but are also noted for their delicious, clove-like fragrance. They bloom over a long period and are justly prized as cut flowers. As the tufted foliage is evergreen, dianthus is also useful as a border plant.

In regions having hot summers, dianthus should be treated as a biennial. Most dianthus varieties will grow in ordinary, well-drained soil in a sunny location. Propagation is by seeds, cuttings, and division.

Purple Coneflower (Echinacea purpurea)

The purple coneflower is a true North American native. He discovered America long before Columbus. This member of the daisy family bears its large, rosy-purple flowers with their prominent, cone-like centers in July and August.

The garden varieties of this tough little customer are very drought resistant, making them very useful in hot, dry climates. The long-lasting, bright-colored flowers, somewhat resembling sunflowers, are borne on long stems in late summer and early fall.

This perennial does best in full sun, but may be grown in light shade. Plant about 2 feet apart. Plants may be started by division or root cuttings made in spring or early fall.

Plantain Lily (Hosta)

Hostas have attractive lily-like blossoms, but are chiefly valued for their mounds of decorative foliage. They are particularly useful for growing in beds or as borders in moist shaded positions. Hosta undulata is a variegated type having green leaves conspicuously splashed with white. Hostas grow from 18 to 36 inches tall, and the leaves are large and lance-shaped. Flowers, according to variety, are lilac-blue or white and are produced on long spikes which stand well above the foliage.

Seeds may be sown in a shaded frame in June. Thin them to stand 2 inches apart, and keep them in the coldframe until the following spring. Plant them into the nursery bed until they are large enough for their permanent location.

Division of established clumps is also used as a means of propagation.

PLANTAIN LILY

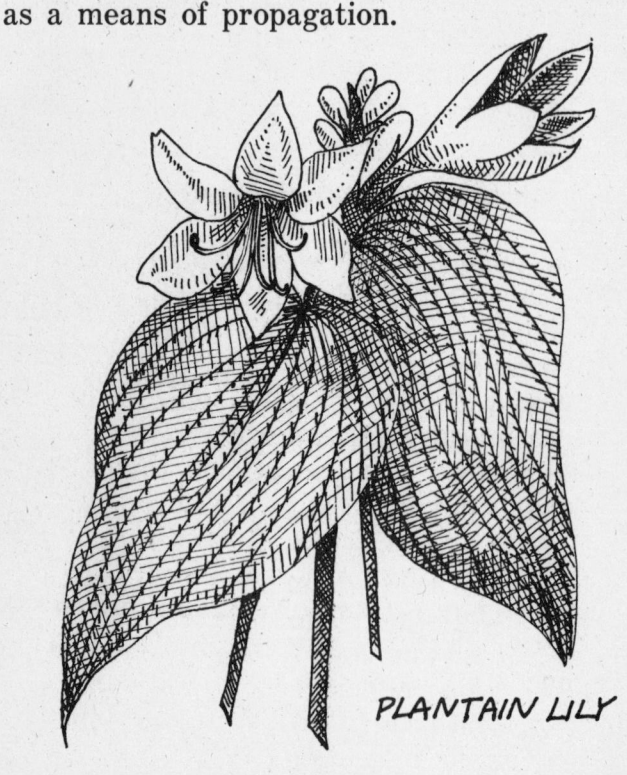

Phlox

Phlox is a North American native. The name itself comes from the Greek word for flame, and this bright, much-loved perennial truly lives up to its name. Any flower which is not only beautiful but fragrant as well is greatly and rightly prized.

Not the least of this plant's virtues is the ease with which it may be cultivated. All the many varieties of phlox will grow in good, fertile garden soil and are equally at home in full sun or light shade.

Phlox may be propagated by seeding or division of the clumps. It is available in a wide variety of colors, some of which have contrasting eyes.

Primroses

Cultivated primroses are among the loveliest of our garden flowers and come in a wide range of colors, including creamy white, rose, copper, chestnut red, rose purple, deep blue, and yellow.

Primroses grown in the garden need shade and moist, rich loam to perform at their very best. They may be found in many different heights, according to the variety preferred. The stems rise from a rosette of thick, leathery, evergreen leaves.

Start primroses from seed by planting them in February in shallow boxes or pans in a mixture of sand, loam and leafmold. The young plants may be set out in the open in May. Primrose clumps may also be dug and divided.

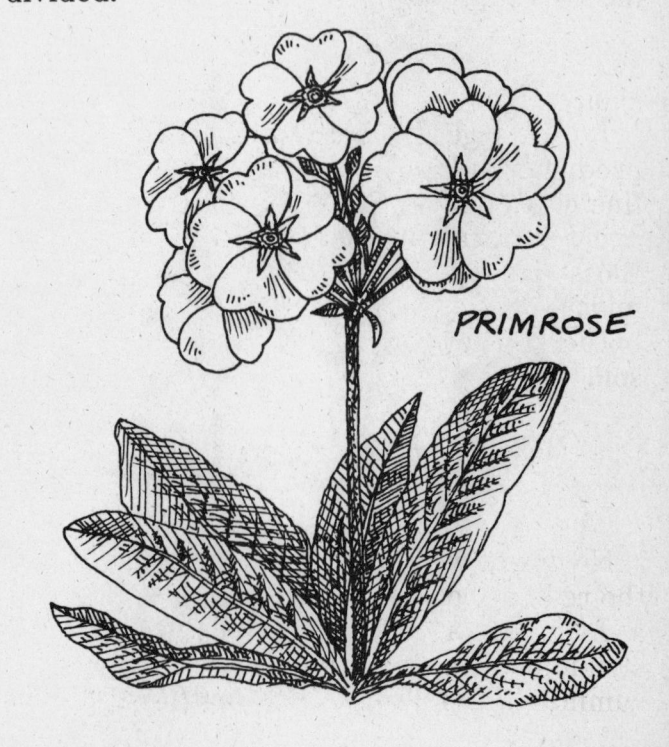

PRIMROSE

Pansies and Violas (Viola)

Pansies have come a long way. The pansy is a descendant of viola tricolor, a wild species. Pansies are of less compact growth than violas, and the flowers are usually much, much larger. And they are available in many vivid colors.

Most popular of all today are the Swiss giants, admired everywhere for their exquisite colors and huge size. Their color tendency is toward the jewel-like shades you might find in a cathedral window. These are nicely balanced by a wide range of yellows, whites and blues, giving the modern gardener who fancies pansies a tremendous choice.

In the larger strains, the huge flowers are produced on long, erect stems, making them fine cutting material for indoor use. Pansies are generally treated as biennials. Blossoming profusely from early spring to midsummer, they are fine for beds and borders. They prefer light shade and moist soil.

Red-Hot Poker (Kniphofia)

No flower was ever more aptly named than the red-hot poker. The plant grows from 3 to 4 feet tall and produces a profusion of strikingly handsome blooms from early summer until fall. The foot-long cones of gay, orange-scarlet, tubular flowers, are very effective along a garden border. Red-hot pokers are another flower greatly beloved by hummingbirds. Their leaves are often 3 feet long, grass-like and somewhat coarse.

The original red-hot pokers were yellow with fiery red tips, but there are now many new varieties, equally hardy, in a great variety of colors.

Alcazar has velvety rose-red spires; Golden Sceptre is a golden yellow; and White Giant has towering spikes of creamy ivory with very large individual blooms.

The plants are usually started from rhizomes. They should be planted outdoors in May with a space of about 15 inches between the plants. Red-hot pokers are hardy in the South, but farther north they may have to be lifted and stored over winter; otherwise they are very easy to grow and present no problems.

Sedum (The Stonecrops)

Sedums are useful for just about every garden purpose — walls, borders, beds and rock gardens. Many gardeners also enjoy them in window boxes and green-houses during the cooler months of the year.

One of the reasons for their popularity is their lofty indifference to their location. They are very good plants for poor soil. Plant them where nothing else will grow. Crevices in a flagstone path or in an old stone wall are among the places sedums will be happy to call home.

Sedums are probably the easiest perennial of all to propagate. You can take up the clumps, divide and replant them at almost any time of the year. Single shoots casually stuck in the soil will take root and grow. Many of the sedums have unusual and interesting leaves. Some varieties even take on brilliant coloring in fall and winter. I know it sounds mean, but this color is likely to be even brighter if the plants are starved for nutrients. Those grown in poor soil, in a walk or on an old wall will be the showiest.

Try some sedums in an earthenware jar and just see what an attractive display they put on for you. Consult a good gardening encyclopedia for a listing of the many different varieties.

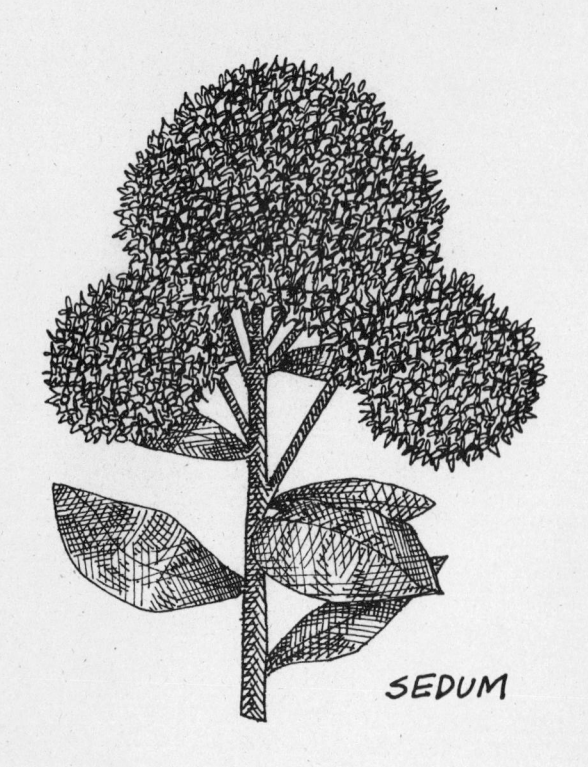

Wild Senna (Cassia Marilandica)

Wild senna is a native perennial herb with an unobtrusive little yellow flower, blooming in midsummer. In its preferred enviroment, moist open situations and swamps, the clumps are very attractive. The small flowers are a bright gold with chocolate-colored anthers. They cluster near the top of the handsome, shrub-like plant, which grows some 3 to 5 feet high.

The light-green leaves are fern-like, and it is the attractive foliage as well as the flowers which make it important garden material, useful in the back of the border or for naturalizing in the woodland.

You may increase your stock by inserting shoots in pots of sandy soil in March. When rooted, place in 3-inch pots, potting on to 5-inch pots, and eventually planting outdoors in their permanent locations.

Wallflowers (Cheiranthus)

Being called a wallflower is a compliment in disguise, for wallflowers are very attractive. However, they are, at least in the United States, somewhat retiring in disposition. They prefer a cool, moist climate, and our hot, dry summers are not very conducive to vigorous growth. They fare much better in England, where they are grown extensively and successfully.

If your climate is suitable and you would like to grow them, plant the seeds outdoors in late spring in a finely prepared seedbed which has had some lime mixed into the soil. Sow the seed thinly and barely cover.

Depending on the area, wallflowers are grown as annuals, biennials or perennials. There are now many named varieties and a wide range of fine color selections.

ADD THESE OUTSTANDING BOOKS TO YOUR GARDEN LIBRARY
AT ONLY $1.95 EACH

America's Master Gardener, Jerry Baker, shows you how to have the garden of your dreams. Easy-to-follow directions and large, clear pictures make these the perfect books for beginners as well as experienced gardeners. Each book in the series covers a different garden subject and each one is chock-full of facts and the know-how to help you make friends with your garden.

IN THIS SERIES

Make Friends with Your Lawn—21558
Basic advice on lawn care, including mowing, watering, fertilizing, and weed and pest control. The book also contains plans for building a new lawn and for rebuilding an old lawn.

Make Friends with Your Annuals—21559
How to select annuals for specific purposes, how to grow from seed, and how to cultivate and protect. The book includes an invaluable list of annuals with descriptions, illustrations and cultural requirements.

Make Friends with Your Evergreens and Ground Covers—21560
How to choose evergreens for beauty and economy, and how to plant, feed and care for them. Basic information on landscaping or re-landscaping.

Make Friends with Your Fruit Trees—21561
Fruit trees to provide shade, natural fences, or patio decoration. Good cultural practices and pruning advice. There is detailed information on the most popular fruits and on nuts, grapes and berries.

Make Friends with Your Vegetable Garden—21562
Where to place the garden, how to make a garden plan, tools and equipment needed, and everything else you'll need to know for the vegetable garden of your dreams. A special section on how to grow and dry herbs.

Make Friends with Your Roses—21563
How to choose the right roses for your garden. Also included is detailed information on soil preparation, setting the plants, cultivating, pruning and propagating new plants.

Make Friends with Your Flowering Shrubs—21652
A fact-filled guide to choosing and caring for these beautiful shrubs. Features a special list showing height at maturity, geographical zone, and other vital information.

Make Friends with Your Perennials and Biennials—21653
This useful guide tells how to naturalize perennials in meadows, shady spots and marshy areas, and how to plan and care for a perennial garden. An unusual section on biennials offers hard-to-find advice on these two-year favorites.

Make Friends with Your House Plants—21654
A complete guide to indoor gardening, including facts about soil, pots and potting, fertilizer, watering, and propagating. A section on decorating with plants adds valuable pointers for showing plants off to their best effect.

Make Friends with Your Shade Trees—21655
A valuable guide to selecting the right trees for your yard and budget. The book includes advice on landscaping, planting, feeding, and general tree care.

Make Friends with Your Flowering Trees—21656
A wealth of information on landscaping, good planting practices and tree care. Features a list to help you pick your trees according to color, size and shape.

Make Friends with Your Bulbs—21657
A detailed guide to choosing the right bulbs for your garden, for every season and location.

Mail this no-risk form today

To Your Bookseller or
Simon and Schuster, Publishers — Dept. BR
630 Fifth Avenue
New York, N.Y. 10020

Please send me the book(s) checked. I enclose payment with the understanding that any book(s) may be returned within one month for full refund.

Name_____

Address_____

City_____State_____Zip_____

$_____ENCLOSED.

Please check books wanted—at $1.95 each
☐ MAKE FRIENDS WITH YOUR LAWN—21558
☐ MAKE FRIENDS WITH YOUR ANNUALS—21559
☐ MAKE FRIENDS WITH YOUR EVERGREENS AND GROUND COVERS—21560
☐ MAKE FRIENDS WITH YOUR FRUIT TREES—21561
☐ MAKE FRIENDS WITH YOUR VEGETABLE GARDEN—21562
☐ MAKE FRIENDS WITH YOUR ROSES—21563
☐ MAKE FRIENDS WITH YOUR FLOWERING SHRUBS—21652
☐ MAKE FRIENDS WITH YOUR PERENNIALS AND BIENNIALS—21653
☐ MAKE FRIENDS WITH YOUR HOUSE PLANTS—21654
☐ MAKE FRIENDS WITH YOUR SHADE TREES—21655
☐ MAKE FRIENDS WITH YOUR FLOWERING TREES—21656
☐ MAKE FRIENDS WITH YOUR BULBS—21657